The Beta Equilibrium, Stability, and Transport Codes

Applications to the Design of Stellarators

PERSPECTIVES IN PHYSICS

Huzihiro Araki, J.A. Libchaber, and Giorgio Parisi, editors

The Beta Equilibrium, Stability, and Transport Codes

Applications to the Design of Stellarators

Frances Bauer
Courant Institute
of Mathematical Sciences
New York University
New York, New York

Paul Garabedian
Courant Institute
of Mathematical Sciences
New York University
New York, New York

Octavio Betancourt
Department of Computer
Sciences
City College of New York
New York, New York

Masahiro Wakatani
Plasma Physics Laboratory
Kyoto University
Kyoto, Japan

ACADEMIC PRESS, INC.
Harcourt Brace Jovanovich, Publishers

Boston Orlando San Diego
New York Austin London Sydney
Tokyo Toronto

ACADEMIC PRESS, INC.
Orlando, Florida 32887

United Kingdom Edition published by
ACADEMIC PRESS INC. (LONDON) LTD.
24-28 Oval Road, London NW1 7DX

Library of Congress Cataloging-in-Publication Data
The Beta equilibrium, stability, and transport codes.

(Perspectives in physics)
Includes bibliographical references and index.
1. Stellarators—Experiments—Data processing.
2. Coding theory.   I. Bauer, Frances.   II. Series.
QC791.77.S7B48   1987   539.7'64   87-1344
ISBN 0-12-082815-4

87 88 89 90   9 8 7 6 5 4 3 2 1
Printed in the United States of America

PREFACE

This book is the outgrowth of a collaboration between the Courant Institute at New York University and the Plasma Physics Laboratory at Kyoto University on the application of the BETA computer codes to the Heliotron E plasma confinement experiment. Numerous examples showing how to use the codes are presented together with a detailed account and listing of the most recent transport code. The work has been supported by the U. S. Department of Energy under Grant DE-FG02-86ER53223 and the National Science Foundation under Grant DMS-8320430. Many of the transport calculations were performed on the Cray X-MP/48 at the San Diego Supercomputer Center. The longer nonlinear stability computations were done on the Fujitsu VP-200 at Nagoya University. We are indebted to Y. Abe for his contributions to that effort. C. Engle prepared the typescript from which the book has been photocopied. We take this opportunity to thank K. Peters and W. Sribney of Academic Press Boston for making possible its publication.

New York and Kyoto   F. Bauer

March 1987   O. Betancourt

              P. Garabedian

              M. Wakatani

TABLE OF CONTENTS

I. INTRODUCTION

1. History of the codes

The BETA equilibrium and stability code has been published in a book [4] that includes substantial documentation, and it has been made available to the user community at the National Magnetic Fusion Energy Computer Center in Livermore. However, experience has shown that it is no easy matter to prepare an input file for the code in cases of more complicated stellarator configurations. We therefore present in this book a dozen input files that have been developed to model some of the more significant stellarator experiments of current interest. We also include a listing of the BETA neoclassical transport code that performs a Monte Carlo calculation of the confinement time using files from the equilibrium code. This computational data is all described in the context of the relevant physics.

The equilibrium code is based on a finite element formulation of the variational principle of ideal magnetohydrodynamics [3]. The calculation is implemented in a flux coordinate system that presumes the existence of a nested family of toroidal magnetic surfaces. An ergodic flux constraint is imposed on the pressure p. Approximate solutions are found whose dependence on the mesh size must be examined carefully. The solution only exists in a weak sense, so that the approximation improves asymptotically as the mesh size decreases toward some positive limit below which incompatibilities associated with the KAM theory of dynamical systems are expected to appear.

Nonlinear stability is analyzed by performing a second minimization of the energy subject to a linear constraint that depends on the choice of a test function. The test function is selected from information concerning the mode whose stability is under investigation. It is necessary to make careful convergence studies in order to distinguish

1

physical instability from the truncation error. The energy landscape is so flat that it becomes necessary in examples of practical interest to estimate it to seven or eight significant digits. This requires a substantial allotment of computer capacity, but the situation can be improved by vectorization in the toroidal direction.

The equilibrium and stability code incorporates a reliable computation of the Mercier local stability criterion. This is evaluated conveniently in terms of the flux coordinates that occur in our formulation of the variational principle. Fourier coefficients of the series used to represent the magnetic field strength B and the parallel current λ can be used to assess quantitatively the incompatibilities that are associated with nonexistence of a solution. Likewise a simplified theory of transport is used to calculate a geometric confinement time τ whose properties are related to the Mercier criterion [8].

The Monte Carlo transport code that we list in Chapter V has been written to use output files from the equilibrium calculation [5]. It implements the method of Boozer and Kuo-Petravic [12] in flux coordinates. Exponential rates of decay of expected values of integrals of the solution of a drift kinetic equation provide estimates of the confinement time for both ions and electrons. The fast algorithm that is used facilitates computation of the electron losses. Spectral analysis of the distribution functions for the ions and electrons enable us to impose the requirement for charge neutrality in a practical fashion at low collision frequencies. Fourier coefficients in a representation of the electric potential are used to solve suitable quasineutrality equations numerically. In this way an attempt is made to explain anomalous electron transport as the consequence of resonance in the electric field and to justify using the ion confinement time without an electric field to estimate energy and particle confinement times [6]. The model seems to be consistent with recent experimental data about losses through the electron channel.

There are several versions of the BETA equilibrium, stability and transport codes. The earliest work was concerned with sharp boundary models in two and three dimensions that only involved solutions of Laplace's equation [7]. In 1978 we published a book that listed the first successful equilibrium code for a diffuse plasma in three dimensions without two-dimensional symmetry [3]. Herrnegger [18] has made extensive use of that version of the BETA code to perform parameter studies at the Max Planck Institute for Plasma Physics in Garching. It is quite robust, but there are difficulties with convergence of the magnetic axis which become visible as small and almost negligible errors in its location for an exact axially symmetric solution.

This difficulty has been overcome in a later version published in 1984 that has been written to treat the problems of both nonlinear and local stability [4]. The latter version is discussed in this book and is available for general usage at the National Magnetic Fusion Energy Computer Center. It has been adapted by Y. Abe of Nagoya University to run on the Fujitsu VP-200 computer [1]. To that end he has made significant modifications of the vectorization. This code has also been used by J. Nuehrenberg and R. Zille at Garching in the design of the Helias configuration [26]. Both the Mercier criterion and a simplified expression for confinement time are included as output. Files that are created by the newer equilibrium code provide the data that are used as input to the BETA neoclassical transport code.

There are two further versions of the BETA equilibrium code that address the issue of existence of magnetic islands. The first of these replaces the islands by current sheets that are perhaps not physically realistic. A later spectral code now under development treats the magnetic islands by means of a representation of the magnetic field due to Marcal [23] and Boozer [10]. Fig. 1 displays the magnetic islands calculated with a preliminary version of this code in two dimensions.

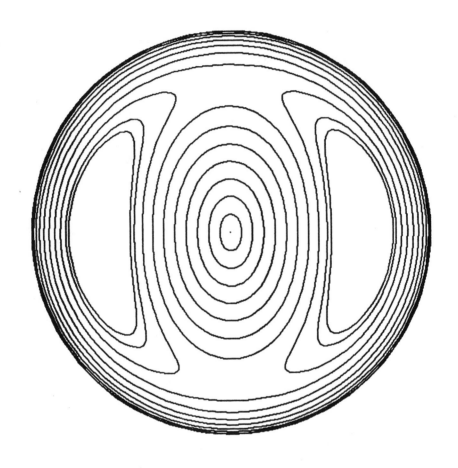

Fig. 1. Equilibrium with islands calculated by the spectral method in two dimensions using a formulation of the variational principle that is not restricted to nested magnetic surfaces.

2. Design of new stellarator experiments

In Japan a design study for a large new helical system has been started as a joint project involving several universities. The purpose of the project is to confine a high temperature plasma with relevance to reactors and with a long pulse discharge, and to develop an understanding of plasma physics in such a regime. The minor radius should be 50 or 60 cm, with aspect ratio between 7 and 9, and the magnetic field is supposed to be about 4 tesla. Optimization of transport becomes an important issue, with the hope of achieving an energy confinement time above 100 ms at an average temperature of 5 keV. Improvement of the β limit to a range between 3% and 5% is sought. Primary effort is going into the investigation of a device with an $\ell = 2$ helical winding comparable to that of the Heliotron E. Since the BETA codes are capable of examining three-dimensional magnetohydrodynamic equilibrium at finite β, nonlinear stability of global modes, Mercier stability against local modes, and neoclassical confinement time for both ions and electrons, they have been employed in this major design study.

The equilibrium, stability and transport codes, together with line tracing techniques, seem to provide an adequate theory with which to design new stellarator experiments. However, the search for desirable configurations remains open. One would like to achieve β limits for equilibrium and nonlinear stability of at least 5% or 10%. No more than a moderate violation of the Mercier local stability criterion $\Omega \geq 0$ should be tolerated. Major resonances are to be avoided and it is necessary to maintain well defined magnetic surfaces s = const. over the full range of β that occurs. There ought to be adequate shear $\iota' = \iota'(s)$, and the rotational transform ι should not change much with β. A geometric confinement time τ well over 100 appears to be needed. Moreover, at the dimensionless collision frequency $\bar{\nu} = 1$ of a typical reactor regime the electron confinement time τ_e should be larger than

5

the ion confinement time τ_i when the electric field is put equal to zero. If these specifications are not met the prospects for a successful reactor are poor.

The Heliac described in Section II.9 is a candidate for a reactor that meets most of our requirements, but its aspect ratio A = 30 is too big for an intermediate experiment. The ℓ = -1,2 stellarator mentioned in Section II.11 is a more reasonable example to propose, but the advantage of minimal parallel current is offset by a small magnetic hill V"/V' > 0. It is not easy to find a satisfactory winding law for the more complicated Helias. The success of conventional designs like the ATF-1 will be decided by the outcome of that experiment, but the prognosis from the codes is not entirely favorable because the Mercier criterion fails noticeably with Ω < -0.3 when β = 0.05, and the geometric confinement time is only 25.

Comparisons of the theory implemented in the BETA codes with the experimental data that is available for stellarators are encouraging. Average β limits of 0.5% for the Wendelstein VII-A and 1.8% for the Heliotron E that have been observed in the laboratory agree well with nonlinear stability calculations. The occurrence of resistive magnetohydrodynamic activity in the Heliotron E at lower values of β is consistent with a negative Mercier criterion in that range. Gross energy confinement times of about 10 ms in the experiments can similarly be reconciled with our Monte Carlo computations.

6

3. List of symbols

a	plasma radius
A	aspect ratio
A_j	polynomial coefficients
A_{jk}	Taylor series coefficients
b_{mn}	Fourier coefficients of $1/B^2$
B	magnetic field
c	speed of light
C_{mn}	Fourier coefficients of charge
d	amplitude
D	Jacobian
e_0	convergence factor
E	potential energy or electric field
E_k	energy of a particle
f, F	distribution functions
g, g_j	test functions
h	mesh size
H	Jacobian
I	net current
i, j, k, ℓ	indices
J	current density
K	scale factor
ℓ_{km}	Fourier coefficients
L	circumference
L_1, L_2, L_3	differential operators
m, n	poloidal and toroidal indices
M	mass
N	number of particles
p	pressure
P_{mn}	Fourier coefficients of electric potential
q	charge

r	radial coordinate
R	radius of flux surface
s	toroidal flux
S	source
t	time
T	temperature distribution
T_e, T_i	electron and ion temperatures
T_{ij}	Maxwell stress tensor
u, v	poloidal and toroidal coordinates
U	diffusive velocity
v	speed of a particle
$v_\parallel$	parallel velocity
V	volume inside flux surface
W	energy
x, y, z	rectangular coordinates
α	atomic mass
β	plasma parameter $2p/B^2$
γ	gas constant
Γ	expected value
δs	island width or step size
δt	collision time step
δW	variation of energy
δ_{ij}	Kronecker delta
Δ_{mn}	Fourier coefficients for boundary
ϵ	scale factor
ζ	Clebsch potential for current
η	magnetic moment cosine $v_\parallel/v$
η_1, η_2	resistivities
θ	toroidal angle
ι	rotational transform
λ	parallel current

8

$\lambda_{\parallel}$	guiding center step size
μ	magnetic moment
ν	collision frequency
$\bar{\nu}$	dimensionless collision frequency
ξ	displacement
ρ_L	gyroradius
$\rho_{\parallel}$	parallel gyroradius
ρ_{mn}	Fourier coefficients of $\rho_{\parallel}$
σ	drift surface or flux function
τ	confinement time
τ_e, τ_i	electron and ion confinement times
ϕ	scalar potential for B
$\tilde{\phi}, \tilde{\psi}$	renormalized angular coordinates
Φ	electric potential
ψ, Ψ	multiple-valued flux functions
ω	growth rate
Ω	measure of Mercier criterion

II. SAMPLE RUNS

In this chapter we present fifteen typical runs of the BETA equilibrium, stability and transport codes. Included with each run is a statement relating the physics of the example to the computational model.

A nonlinear growth rate ω is calculated by comparing the primary minimum value E_0 of the potential energy

$$E = \int \left(\frac{1}{2} B^2 + \frac{p}{\gamma-1}\right) dV$$

with a second minimum value E_1. The second minimiztion is performed over perturbations ξ of the equilibrium that are subject to a linear constraint of the form

$$(\xi, \xi_0) = d \ ,$$

where ξ_0 is a given test function and d is a specified amplitude. The test function ξ_0 is selected from knowledge of the mode whose growth rate is sought. This knowledge usually consists of an exact solution of the eigenvalue problem for a special example with one-dimensional symmetry [3]. After both E_0 and E_1 have been computed on a fixed mesh, the growth rate ω is defined by the Rayleigh quotient

$$- \omega^2 = \frac{\delta W}{\| \xi \|^2} = \frac{E_1 - E_0}{\| \xi \|^2} \ ,$$

where $\| \xi \|$ is a norm related to the kinetic energy. Careful convergence studies are needed to estimate $- \omega^2$ at zero mesh size and to determine whether the stability requirement $\delta W > 0$ is fulfilled (cf. Section 2).

The Mercier criterion $\Omega \geq 0$ is used to assess local stability. We put

$$\Omega = \frac{s}{\pi^2 \iota^2} \, [\Omega_s + \Omega_w + \Omega_\lambda] \ ,$$

where

$$\Omega_s = \frac{(\iota')^2}{4} - \iota' \iint \frac{(J - I'B) \cdot B}{(\nabla s)^2} \, D \ du \ dv$$

is a term measuring the shear ι', where

$$\Omega_w = p' \, [V'' - p' \iint \frac{D \ du \ dv}{B^2} \,] \iint \frac{B^2}{(\nabla s)^2} \, D \ du \ dv$$

is a term measuring the magnetic well $-V''/V'$, and where

$$\Omega_\lambda = [\iint \frac{J \cdot B}{(\nabla s)^2} \, D \ du \ dv]^2 - \iint \frac{B^2}{(\nabla s)^2} \, D \ du \ dv \iint \frac{(J \cdot B)^2}{B^2 (\nabla s)^2} \, D \ du \ dv$$

is a term measuring the parallel current $J \cdot B$. In general Ω is much easier to compute than $-\omega^2$, but its relevance to magnetohydrodynamic stability is less apparent. We conjecture that a very negative value of Ω implies that the magnetic surfaces $s = $ const. have deteriorated and a soft β limit has been reached at which there may be significant losses through the electron channel (cf. Section IV.1). Resistive magneto-hydrodynamic activity seems also to have been observed when $\Omega < 0$.

1. Wendelstein VII-A fixed boundary equilibrium

The Wendelstein VII-A was the first successful major experiment for stellarators without net current. For historical reasons it has an excessively large aspect ratio A = 20 and there is almost no shear. Because of the large aspect ratio growth rates are exceptionally small. Therefore it becomes difficult to do nonlinear stability, which requires eight or more significant figures in the energy for such a case.

Here we present a fixed boundary equilibrium run. For a simple $\ell = 2$ configuration like this there is little difficulty with convergence.

A pressure profile of the form $p = p_0(1-s)$ has been chosen by setting XPR, YPR, and ZPR all equal to 1.0 in the input file. The pressure distribution is such that the Mercier criterion $\Omega \geq 0$ comes out with a very flat, but slightly negative, profile for Ω. This appears to be a physically reasonable choice, since substantial negative values of Ω may indicate resistive instability. The following page shows the input file, and the next page after that is a plot of four equally spaced cross sections of the stellarator in one field period.

Because of the large aspect ratio it was necessary to set SA2 = 8.00 to improve convergence of the ψ equation. We also set ALFU = -0.2 in an attempt to redistribute the mesh equally in the u variable. This is done in Subroutine SURF by means of the transformation

UBAR = UP1 + ALFU*SIN(UP1).

INPUT DATA AS READ FROM INPUT DATA DECK

EP	RBOU	QLZ	NRUN	NGEOM	RUN
0.0500	1.0000	5.0000	1	1	1003

DEL0	DEL1	DEL2	DEL3	DEL10	DEL20	DEL30
0.0000	0.0000	0.3300	0.0000	0.0000	0.0000	0.0000

DEL22	DEL33	DELA	DELB	DELC
0.0000	0.0000	0.0000	0.0000	0.0000

XPR	YPR	ZPR	P0	AMU0	AMU1	AMU2
1.0000	1.0000	1.0000	0.0050	0.1000	0.0000	0.0100

ALF	ALFU
0.5000	-0.2000

NI	NJ	NK	ASYE	ERR
9	16	16	1.0E+03	1.0E-19

SA1	SA2	SA3	DT
4.0000	8.0000	0.0700	0.0220

SE1	SEMU	SEAX
300.00	0.20	2.00

SAFI	NE	NVAC
2.2000	100	-11

NR	NZ	NT	NAC	DPSI	GAM	IGAM
3	2	100	200	0.000	2.000	1

MIS	NIS	NAS	IROT	MF	NF	IPF
1	0	-5	0	4	2	5

IC	ITERF	TLIM
50	10000	800.0

PRINT1	PRINT2	PRINT3	PRINT4	PRINT5	PRINT6	PRINT7	PRINT8
AX ERR	RO ERR	PSI ERR		FPSIROAX ERR	JAC RAT	DELENER	ENERGY

US0	UIN	USM	IVAX	BULGE	TILT	COIL
0.0000	0.0000	0.0000	0	0.0000	0.0000	0.0000

NIV	NV	NP	OM	SAFV	SE4	C1	C2
1	0	0	0.0000	0.0000	0.0000	0.0000	0.0000

KW1	KW2	AK3	TORS	AMPH	EVERT	WRAD	VERT
0	0	0.0000	0.0000	0.0000	0.0000	0.0000	0.0000

NRA1	NRA2	NZA1	NZA2	MK1	MK2	MK3	MK4
1	3	1	2	11	21	31	10

EL1	EL2	EM1	EM2	M	N
0.0000	0.0000	0.0000	0.0000	0	0

EAM1	EAM2	EAM3	EAM4	EAM5	EAM6
0.0000	0.0000	0.0000	0.0000	0.0000	0.0000

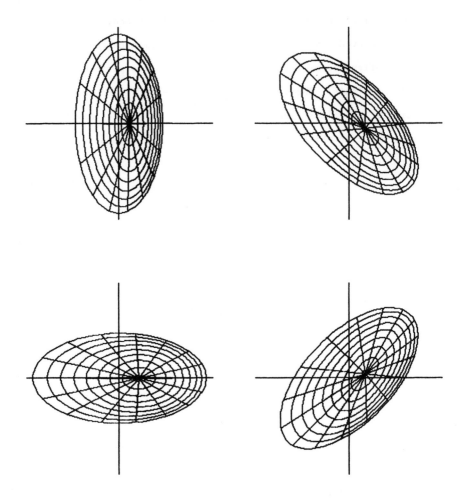

Fig. 2. Four cross sections at v = 0.00, 0.25, 0.50, 0.75, EP = 0.05, QLZ = 5 of the flux surfaces in one field period of the Wendelstein VII-A experiment as they appear plotted by the BETA equilibrium code. Also shown are coordinate rays u = const.

2. Wendelstein VII-AS nonlinear stability test

The Wendelstein VII-AS is a recent modification of the Wendelstein VII-A experiment designed to reduce the Pfirsch-Schlueter current λ. This is achieved by introducing multiple harmonics that result in a complex configuration for which it is hard to perform a nonlinear stability analysis. There are five field periods, and the rotational transform ι is almost uniformly equal to 0.4. We have devised a stability test in which additional field periods of identical shape are added to bring the total rotational transform up to unity, so that the simplest m = 1 mode becomes resonant. This is a somewhat academic mathematical mode because of overlap in the geometry, but it serves as an adequate test for nonlinear stability if we assume that all resonant modes have the same critical value of $\beta = 2<p>/<B^2>$.

In the present example NRUN = 12 field periods are used to calculate the increment δW of the energy at $\beta = 0.01$ on a mesh of 12×24×48×12 points. After careful extrapolation to zero mesh size h = 0 using the rule

$$\delta W = A_0 + A_2 h^2 + A_3 h^3 \ ,$$

we found that the mode is stable at $\beta = 0.01$ with $\delta W = 0.001 > 0$. The case is exceptionally difficult, so the run required 18700 iterations for equilibrium and 17000 iterations for stability. It was made on the Cray 2 and took 21 hours of CPU time. These numbers are not typical and reflect the unusual difficulty. In addition to the following two pages of input for the run and a plot of the rather distorted cross sections, we include a diagram showing the dependence of the Mercier quantity Ω on the form of the pressure profile.

For this example NGEOM = 4, which permits a representation of the outer surface by means of parameters in the first four cards of the

15

input file. Here we have redistributed the coordinate system in u by setting ALFU = -0.125. The plot of the cross sections in Fig. 3 shows that the mesh is nearly equally spaced. The SA1 and SA2 values are bigger than those for the Wendelstein VII-A because of the large distortions. In order to improve the resolution for this complicated geometry the grid was chosen to have twice as many intervals in the v direction as in the u direction. The overall process was slowed down, but the convergence was improved further by choosing a small artificial time step DT. After making adjustments the convergence became adequate, but the runs required many iterations as indicated by the numbers given above.

This example illustrates an m = 1 stability run with DPSI = 0.1. The test function for stability is a vector with components δR cos(mu-nv), $\delta\psi$ sin(mu-nv), δr_0cos nv and δz_0sin nv specifying perturbations of R, ψ, r_0 and z_0 that are defined in Subroutine SURF by means of the input parameters EL1,... and EAM1,... listed on Cards 36 and 38 of the input file (cf. Section III.1). It should be noted that for NGEOM = 4 the input data file consists of 40 lines instead of the usual 38.

EP	RBOU	QLZ	NRUN	NGEOM	RUN
0.1111	1.0000	5.0000	12	4	1003

DEL1R	DEL1Z	DEL20	DEL30	DEL40	DEL21	DEL31
0.3000	0.0000	0.3500	-0.0600	0.0000	0.3300	0.0300

DEL41	DEL22	DEL32	DEL42	DEL23	DEL33	DEL43
0.0100	-0.0200	-0.0300	-0.0100	0.0400	0.0000	0.0000

DEL0	ALFU2	ALFU3
-0.0900	0.0000	0.0000

XPR	YPR	ZPR	P0	AMU0	AMU1	AMU2
2.0000	1.0000	1.0000	0.0150	0.1000	0.0000	0.0000

ALF	ALFU
1.0000	-0.1250

NI	NJ	NK	ASYE	ERR
13	24	48	1.0E+03	1.0E-19

SA1	SA2	SA3	DT
6.0000	12.0000	0.0700	0.0090

SE1	SEMU	SEAX
300.00	0.40	6.00

SAFI	NE	NVAC
2.2000	100	-11

NR	NZ	NT	NAC	DPSI	GAM	IGAM
3	2	-18700	400	0.100	2.000	1

MIS	NIS	NAS	IROT	MF	NF	IPF
1	0	-5	0	6	3	7

IC	ITERF	TLIM
100	35000	80000.0

PRINT1	PRINT2	PRINT3	PRINT4	PRINT5	PRINT6	PRINT7	PRINT8
AX ERR	RO ERR	PSI ERR	FPSIRO	AX ERR	JAC RAT	DELENER	ENERGY

US0	UIN	USM	IVAX	BULGE	TILT	COIL
0.0000	0.0000	0.0000	0	0.0000	0.0000	0.0000

NIV	NV	NP	OM	SAFV	SE4	C1	C2
1	0	0	0.0000	0.0000	0.0000	0.0000	0.0000

KW1	KW2	AK3	TORS	AMPH	EVERT	WRAD	VERT
0	0	0.0000	0.0000	0.0000	0.0000	0.0000	0.0000

NRA1	NRA2	NZA1	NZA2	MK1	MK2	MK3	MK4
1	3	1	2	11	21	31	10

EL1	EL2	EM1	EM2	M	N
1.0000	0.0000	1.0000	0.0000	1	1

EAM1	EAM2	EAM3	EAM4	EAM5	EAM6
2.0000	0.0000	0.0000	-1.0000	0.0000	0.0000

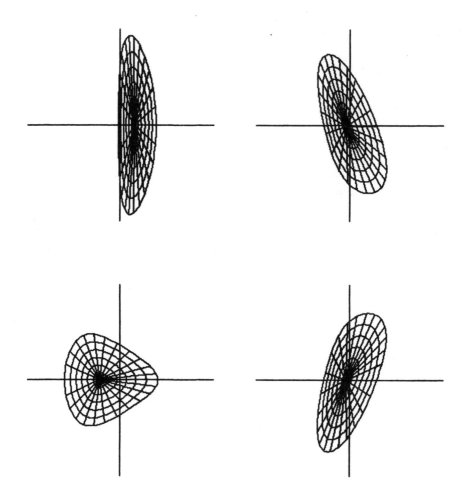

CROSS SECTIONS AT V= .00,.25,.50,.75, 1/(EP•QLZ)= 1.80
MAJOR RADIUS= 9.00   MINOR RADIUS= 1.00

Fig. 3.   Flux surfaces and coordinate rays of the Wendelstein VII-AS.

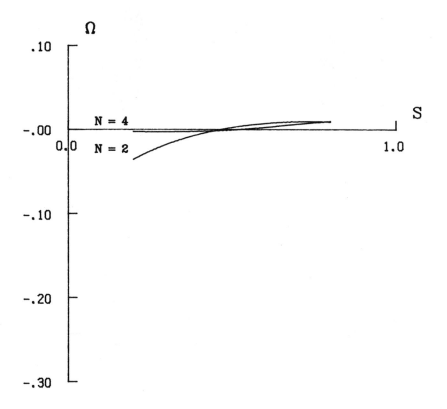

Fig. 4. Calculation of the term Ω that appears in the Mercier criterion showing its dependence on the pressure profile for $\beta = 0.007$. The Mercier criterion is plotted for the Wendelstein VII-AS with EP = 0.1, QLZ = 5, and $p = p_0(1 - s^{N/2})^2$.

3. Heliotron E stability for an m = 2 mode

The Heliotron E is one of the biggest and most successful stellarator experiments to date. Results from the BETA codes are in good agreement with a critical average β = 0.018 and a gross energy confinement time τ_E = 10 ms that have been achieved in the laboratory. A value of ι = 1 for the rotational transform that occurs inside the plasma creates a significant resonance for the m = n = 1, m = n = 2, ... modes. Finer radial resolution is required for a successful study of the nonlinear stability of these modes. This is accomplished in the BETA code by restricting the computation to the interior of a flux tube just enclosing the resonant surface. Such an approach is successful because energy perturbations scale like the fourth power of the plasma radius. As a result the calculation of δW can be dominated by truncation errors from the outer shell. Bringing the wall inside the plasma region is equivalent to making a perturbation that vanishes outside the resonant layer, which is consistent with theoretical knowledge about the eigenfunction.

The present example is drawn from a series of runs for an m = 2 mode of such an inner tube of the Heliotron E plasma restricted to s ≤ 0.6. In addition to the usual page of input and a plot of cross sections, a diagram showing the dependence of the inner tube growth rate ω of the m = 1 and m = 2 modes on β is displayed. This demonstrates that the critical β for the m = 1 mode agrees well with the experimental value, as has been shown in previous publications [4]. The results for the m = 1 mode shown in Fig. 6 were checked at very fine mesh sizes on the Fujitsu VP-200 computer at Nagoya [31]. Nonlinear stability runs on that machine are almost as fast as corresponding equilibrium runs because vectorization becomes very effective for the large vector length NK*NRUN that occurs in the v direction. Fig. 7 is a plot of the Mercier criterion at the critical value β = 0.018 which establishes that an average Ω = -0.02 can occur in an actual experiment.

Comparison with experimental data suggests that the Mercier criterion may give a valid prediction of resistive magnetohydrodynamic activity below the soft β limit.

To implement the inner tube concept we have set EP = 0.0769, DEL2 = 0.27 and ZPR = 0.6. For the m = 2 mode we put NRUN = 9, whereas for the m = 1 mode we put NRUN = 18. We set the parameter ALF in the input file equal to 0.5 for all fixed boundary runs and find that this gives the best distribution of the radial coordinate. We have studied the tuning of the various parameters in order to improve convergence, but the Heliotron E case is relatively simple. Starting the acceleration at a later point in the iteration scheme can help to get a run launched, and that is done by increasing NAC. Difficulty with initial displacements can be improved by increasing SE1 to 600.

This run is concerned with stability of an m = 2 mode for which EAM2 = 2.0 and EAM5 = -1.0, with all other constants in the test function modeling the mode set equal to zero. The test function used to study stability can be varied, but should satisfy the relation

$$\delta\psi = -\frac{1}{m}\frac{d(s\delta R)}{ds} \, ,$$

where m is the mode number and $\delta\psi$ and δR are coefficients of the trigonometric functions in the perturbations of ψ and R defined in Section 2. Theory suggests that δR should change sign at the resonant surface where ι = n/m, but in practice it is more effective to restrict the computation to an inner tube as described above. We note again that extrapolation to zero mesh size in the stability study should be done by fitting the data with a cubic polynomial [4]. A better implementation of the inner tube concept that has been carried out quite recently leads to a β limit of only 1% for the internal m = 1 mode.

21

INPUT DATA AS READ FROM INPUT DATA DECK

EP	RBOU	QLZ	NRUN	NGEOM	RUN
0.0769	1.0000	18.0000	9	1	1010

DEL0	DEL1	DEL2	DEL3	DEL10	DEL20	DEL30
0.0000	0.0000	0.2700	0.0000	0.0000	0.0000	0.0000

DEL22	DEL33	DELA	DELB	DELC
0.0000	0.0000	0.0000	0.0000	0.0000

XPR	YPR	ZPR	P0	AMU0	AMU1	AMU2
2.0000	1.0000	0.6000	0.0300	0.0300	0.0000	0.0300

ALF	ALFU
0.5000	0.0000

NI	NJ	NK	ASYE	ERR
13	24	24	1.0E+03	1.0E-17

SA1	SA2	SA3	DT
4.0000	4.0000	0.5000	0.0100

SE1	SEMU	SEAX
300.00	0.10	2.00

SAFI	NE	NVAC
2.2000	50	-11

NR	NZ	NT	NAC	DPSI	GAM	IGAM
1	1	-7600	200	0.050	2.000	1

MIS	NIS	NAS	IROT	MF	NF	IPF
1	0	-5	0	6	3	7

IC	ITERF	TLIM
50	14000	7200.0

PRINT1	PRINT2	PRINT3	PRINT4	PRINT5	PRINT6	PRINT7	PRINT8
AX ERR	RO ERR	PSI ERR	MU ERR	OAX ERR	JAC RAT	DELENER	ENERGY

US0	UIN	USM	IVAX	BULGE	TILT	COIL
0.0000	0.0000	0.0000	0	0.0000	0.0000	0.0000

NIV	NV	NP	OM	SAFV	SE4	C1	C2
1	0	0	0.0000	0.0000	0.0000	0.0000	0.0000

KW1	KW2	AK3	TORS	AMPH	EVERT	WRAD	VERT
0	0	0.0000	0.0000	0.0000	0.0000	0.0000	0.0000

NRA1	NRA2	NZA1	NZA2	MK1	MK2	MK3	MK4
1	3	1	2	11	21	32	10

EL1	EL2	EM1	EM2	M	N
0.0000	0.0000	0.0000	0.0000	2	2

EAM1	EAM2	EAM3	EAM4	EAM5	EAM6
0.0000	2.0000	0.0000	0.0000	-1.0000	0.0000

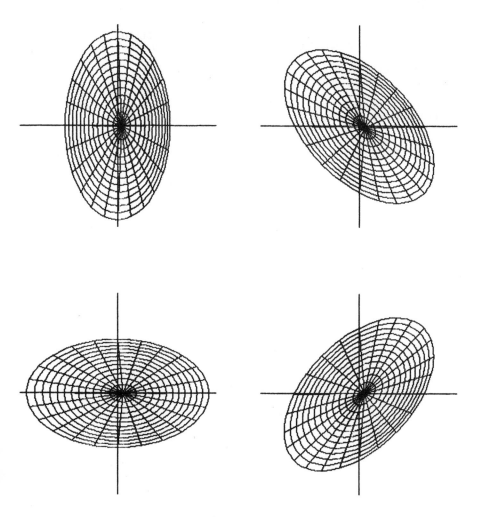

CROSS SECTIONS AT V= .00,.25,.50,.75, 1/(EP∗QLZ)= 0.73
MAJOR RADIUS= 13.14   MINOR RADIUS= 1.00

Fig. 5.   Cross   sections   of   the   flux   surfaces   of   the Heliotron E.

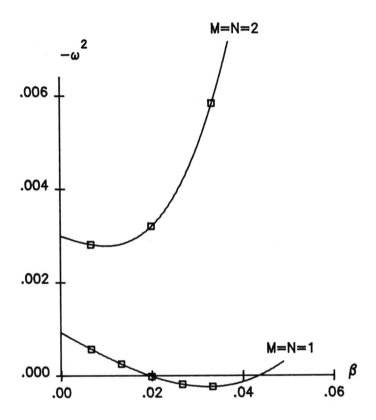

Fig. 6. Growth rates ω of two modes of the Heliotron E. The resolution of the test function is refined in the radial direction by restricting the computation to a region just enclosing the resonant surface where $\iota = 1$. Here we display a nonlinear stability test perturbing an inner flux tube of Heliotron E with EP = 0.077, QLZ = 18, DEL2 = 0.27, and $p = p_0(1 - 0.6s^2)^2$.

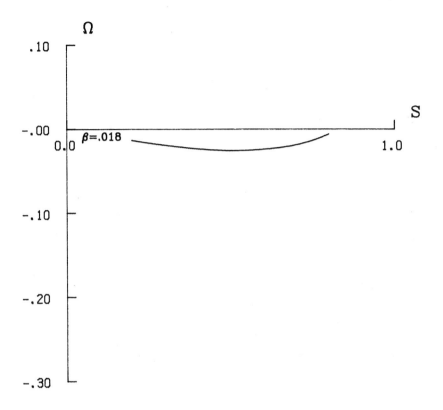

Fig. 7. Computation of the Mercier term Ω showing that it can become negative for a flattened distribution of pressure with high β that has been achieved in the laboratory. The Mercier criterion is plotted for Heliotron E with EP = 0.1, QLZ = 18, DEL2 = 0.3, and $p = p_0(1 - s^2)^1$.

4. Heliotron H free boundary stability

Our model of the Heliotron H represents an early version of a
proposal to upgrade the Heliotron E experiment. We use it to illustrate
how the BETA codes are run to calculate stability for a free boundary m
= 1 mode. In the case of a free boundary the winding law for the
stellarator is formulated as a boundary condition on the scalar
potential ϕ of the magnetic field at an outer control surface. The
corresponding form of the variational principle leads to a theory of
nonlinear stability that is explained elsewhere [4]. In this case the
resolution of our method is limited to six figures of accuracy in the
energy because of incompatibilities that occur in the implementation of
the free boundary condition. This barely suffices to determine stability
in the easiest cases for the m = 1 free surface mode. For the Heliotron
H there is a pronounced ι = 1 resonance near the surface of the plasma
that makes it possible to come to a convincing conclusion. The global
free boundary m = 1 mode turns out to be unstable for β = 0.017 (cf.
[31]).

In the case of free boundary modes extrapolation to zero mesh size
is performed using the quadratic rule

$$\delta W = A_0 + A_2 h^2.$$

The number of radial mesh points NIV in the vacuum is taken equal to
the corresponding value NI in the plasma. When the mesh is refined the
value of the relaxation parameter OM is scaled to behave like $2 - A_1 h$.

INPUT DATA AS READ FROM INPUT DATA DECK

EP	RBOU	QLZ	NRUN	NGEOM	RUN
0.1587	0.4500	15.0000	15	1	1011

DEL0	DEL1	DEL2	DEL3	DEL10	DEL20	DEL30
0.0000	0.0000	0.2200	0.0000	0.0000	0.0000	0.0000

DEL22	DEL33	DELA	DELB	DELC
0.0000	0.0000	0.0000	0.0000	0.0000

XPR	YPR	ZPR	P0	AMU0	AMU1	AMU2
2.0000	1.0000	1.0000	0.0270	0.0687	0.0000	0.0227

ALF	ALFU
0.0000	0.0000

NI	NJ	NK	ASYE	ERR
7	12	12	1.0E+03	1.0E-17

SA1	SA2	SA3	DT
4.0000	4.0000	0.3000	0.0100

SE1	SEMU	SEAX
300.00	0.20	-2.00

SAFI	NE	NVAC
2.2000	50	11

NR	NZ	NT	NAC	DPSI	GAM	IGAM
1	1	-5600	200	0.025	2.000	1

MIS	NIS	NAS	IROT	MF	NF	IPF
1	0	-5	0	4	3	4

IC	ITERF	TLIM
50	10000	4000.0

PRINT1	PRINT2	PRINT3	PRINT4	PRINT5	PRINT6	PRINT7	PRINT8
AX ERR	RO ERR	PSI ERR	BOU ERR	ROAX ERR	VAC ERR	DELENER	ENERGY

US0	UIN	USM	IVAX	BULGE	TILT	COIL
0.0000	0.0000	-1.0000	-1	0.0000	-0.0240	0.0000

NIV	NV	NP	OM	SAFV	SE4	C1	C2
7	3	1	1.6000	2.0000	1.0000	0.0000	2.6380

KW1	KW2	AK3	TORS	AMPH	EVERT	WRAD	VERT
2	1	1.0000	0.0000	-0.3000	-1.0000	1.5000	0.0000

NRA1	NRA2	NZA1	NZA2	MK1	MK2	MK3	MK4
1	3	1	2	11	21	31	10

EL1	EL2	EM1	EM2	M	N
1.0000	0.0000	1.0000	0.0000	1	1

EAM1	EAM2	EAM3	EAM4	EAM5	EAM6
2.0000	0.0000	0.0000	-1.0000	0.0000	0.0000

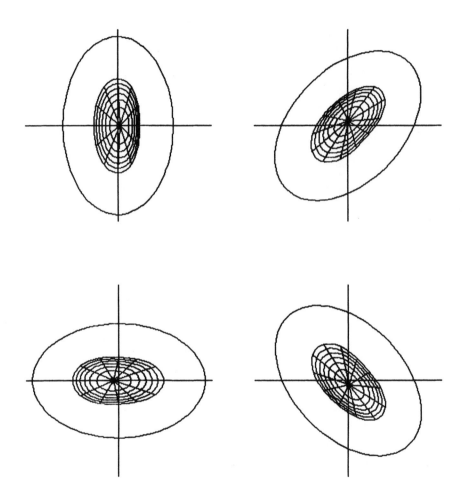

Fig. 8.　Free boundary calculation of a stellarator equilibrium showing
the control surface that surrounds a vacuum field outside the plasma.

5. ATF-1 nonlinear stability test

The ATF-1 is a major conventional $\ell = 2$ stellarator experiment recently constructed at the Oak Ridge National Laboratory. A vertical field is used to access the second stability region. In the BETA code this is modeled by putting DEL3 = 0.05 to introduce an $\ell = 3$ sideband. In an earlier study [4] it was established that this procedure is successful in so far as the m = 3, n = 2 mode is concerned. However, when β increases there is a quite significant change in the profile of the rotational transform. Consequently what appears to be access to the second stability region might instead represent a change in the resonance of the mode under investigation.

One should examine stability for all mode numbers m and n which have resonances $\iota = $ n/m inside the plasma. But since high m requires resolution beyond the practical capability of the code, we study instead a lower mode corresponding to the principal resonances. Thus in the present example we perform a more academic test of the m = 1 mode similar to the one we described for the Wendelstein VII-AS. For each choice of β we add identically shaped field periods to the device so as to achieve a total rotational transform ι as near as possible to unity at the edge of the plasma. For this less realistic configuration we plot the growth rate of the m = 1 mode as a function of the number of field periods NRUN to determine the critical value of β. The nonlinear stability test over many field periods serves to submerge small resonances in one field period so as to analyze the lowest resonant mode of a configuration with significantly longer length scale but no perceptible islands.

Our analysis indicates a good β limit for the ATF-1 experiment in a version given to us by the Oak Ridge National Laboratory with the vertical field included. However, in this configuration it also turns out that the Mercier quantity Ω plunges as low as -0.3 for $\beta = 0.05$, so there may be a difficulty with resistive magnetohydrodynamic activity.

29

INPUT DATA AS READ FROM INPUT DATA DECK

EP	RBOU	QLZ	NRUN	NGEOM	RUN
0.1429	1.0000	12.0000	18	4	1003

DEL1R	DEL1Z	DEL20	DEL30	DEL40	DEL21	DEL31
0.0000	0.0000	0.2000	-0.0600	0.0000	0.2600	0.0300

DEL41	DEL22	DEL32	DEL42	DEL23	DEL33	DEL43
-0.0140	0.0000	0.0000	0.0000	0.0000	0.0000	0.0000

DEL0	ALFU2	ALFU3
-0.0800	0.0000	0.0000

XPR	YPR	ZPR	PO	AMU0	AMU1	AMU2
1.0000	2.0000	1.0000	0.0225	0.0300	0.0000	0.0000

ALF	ALFU
0.5000	-0.3000

NI	NJ	NK	ASYE	ERR
13	24	24	1.0E+03	1.0E-19

SA1	SA2	SA3	DT
4.0000	6.0000	0.5000	0.0100

SE1	SEMU	SEAX
600.00	0.50	4.00

SAFI	NE	NVAC
2.2000	100	-11

NR	NZ	NT	NAC	DPSI	GAM	IGAM
1	1	-10500	200	0.200	2.000	1

MIS	NIS	NAS	IROT	MF	NF	IPF
1	0	-5	0	4	3	7

IC	ITERF	TLIM
100	22000	20000.0

PRINT1	PRINT2	PRINT3	PRINT4	PRINT5	PRINT6	PRINT7	PRINT8
AX ERR	RO ERR	PSI ERR		FPSIROAX ERR	JAC RAT	DELENER	ENERGY

USO	UIN	USM	IVAX	BULGE	TILT	COIL
0.0000	0.0000	0.0000	0	0.0000	0.0000	0.0000

NIV	NV	NP	OM	SAFV	SE4	C1	C2
1	0	0	0.0000	0.0000	0.0000	0.0000	0.0000

KW1	KW2	AK3	TORS	AMPH	EVERT	WRAD	VERT
0	0	0.0000	0.0000	0.0000	0.0000	0.0000	0.0000

NRA1	NRA2	NZA1	NZA2	MK1	MK2	MK3	MK4
1	3	1	2	11	21	31	10

EL1	EL2	EM1	EM2	M	N
1.0000	0.0000	1.0000	0.0000	1	1

EAM1	EAM2	EAM3	EAM4	EAM5	EAM6
2.0000	0.0000	0.0000	-1.0000	0.0000	0.0000

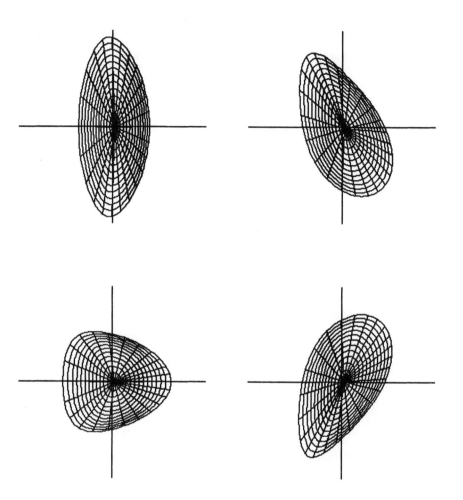

CROSS SECTIONS AT V= .00,.25,.50,.75, 1/(EP*QLZ)= 0.58
MAJOR RADIUS= 7.00   MINOR RADIUS= 1.00

Fig. 9.   Cross sections of the ATF-1 with vertical field coils.

6. Vertical field in the ATF-1 winding law

In the ATF-1 experiment at the Oak Ridge National Laboratory several vertical field coils have been included. Currents in these coils are to be altered as β increases in such a way that the rotational transform ι will not change appreciably. The vertical field coils also serve to add a Δ_{31} harmonic that shifts the magnetic axis outward and stablizes the plasma.

The present run of the vacuum code is part of a study of the effectiveness of the vertical field coils. Modifications of the parameters BULGE, TILT, and COIL have been introduced in Subroutine PBOU so as to represent the boundary values of the scalar potential ϕ = PT of the magnetic field as a Fourier series whose principal terms model the vertical field coils. The terms introduced are of the form C10*SIN(U), C20*SIN(2U) and C30*SIN(3U), where C10 = BULGE, C20 = TILT, and C30 = COIL. Perturbations of an earlier, less satisfactory version of the ATF-1 are considered in which only C10, C20 and C30 are allowed to vary. The run shows that this model does impose on the free boundary a shape similar to that occurring in Section 5. The procedure is effective because there is a diagonally dominant relationship between CM0 and the corresponding free boundary coefficients DELM0. The level curves of ϕ on the outer control surface approximate the shape of the coils, since the jump in the tangential component of $\nabla\phi$ there is perpendicular to the surface current if the field vanishes outside.

The actual updates to Subroutine PBOU for this run are as follows: The seventh line before Statement 70 becomes

        XR1=XR

The fourth line before Statement 70 is replaced by

        Y3=BULGE*SIN(UP1)
        Y4=TILT*SIN(2.*UP1)
        Y5=COIL*SIN(3.*UP1)

Statement 70 becomes

        70 PT(NIV,J,K)=Y2+C2*V+SUM*AMPH+Y3+Y4+Y5

INPUT DATA AS READ FROM INPUT DATA DECK

EP	RBOU	QLZ	NRUN	NGEOM	RUN
0.3176	0.4500	12.0000	1	1	1

DEL0	DEL1	DEL2	DEL3	DEL10	DEL20	DEL30
0.0000	0.0000	0.2300	0.0000	0.0000	0.0000	0.0000

DEL22	DEL33	DELA	DELB	DELC
0.0000	0.0000	0.0000	0.0000	0.0000

XPR	YPR	ZPR	P0	AMU0	AMU1	AMU2
1.0000	1.0000	1.0000	0.0500	0.0300	0.0000	0.0300

ALF	ALFU
0.0000	0.0000

NI	NJ	NK	ASYE	ERR
9	16	16	0.1E+04	0.1E-18

SA1	SA2	SA3	DT
4.0000	4.0000	0.1000	0.0075

SE1	SEMU	SEAX
300.00	0.20	-2.00

SAFI	NE	NVAC
2.0000	100	11

NR	NZ	NT	NAC	DPSI	GAM	IGAM
3	2	100	200	0.000	2.000	1

MIS	NIS	NAS	IROT	MF	NF	IPF
2	0	-5	0	4	3	5

IC	ITERF	TLIM
50	3000	3000.0

PRINT1	PRINT2	PRINT3	PRINT4	PRINT5	PRINT6	PRINT7	PRINT8
AX ERR	RO ERR	PSI ERR	VAC ERR	ROAX ERR	BOU ERR	DELENER	ENERGY

US0	UIN	USM	IVAX	C10	C20	C30
0.0000	0.0000	-1.0000	-1	-0.1200	0.0500	0.0300

NIV	NV	NP	OM	SAFV	SE4	C1	C2
9	3	1	1.6800	2.0000	1.0000	0.0000	1.6500

KW1	KW2	AK3	TORS	AMPH	EVERT	WRAD	VERT
2	1	1.0000	0.0000	-0.3800	-1.0000	1.5000	0.0000

NRA1	NRA2	NZA1	NZA2	MK1	MK2	MK3	MK4
1	3	1	2	11	21	31	10

EL1	EL2	EM1	EM2	M	N
0.0000	0.0000	0.0000	0.0000	0	0

EAM1	EAM2	EAM3	EAM4	EAM5	EAM6
0.0000	0.0000	0.0000	0.0000	0.0000	0.0000

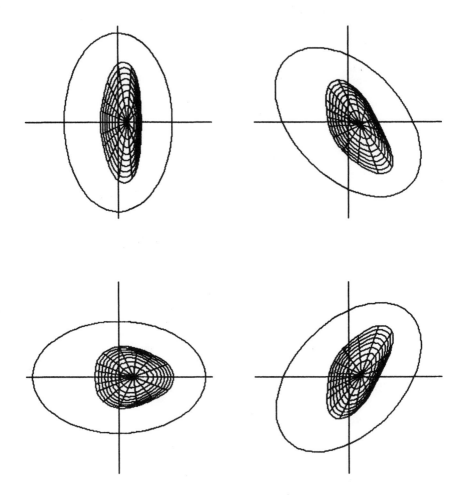

Fig. 10. Free boundary calculation of an ATF-1 configuration in which a winding law to model the vertical field coils has been implemented by prescribing the values of the scalar potential at an outer control surface.

7. Resonant Heliac of small aspect ratio

The Heliac is an $\ell = 1$ stellarator whose cross sections have a pronounced crescent shape that has a stabilizing effect. The helical windings dominate the toroidal field and there is sizable rotational transform in each field period that may lead to dangerous resonances, especially when there is little shear. We present four Heliac examples. The first has a dangerous resonance and low aspect ratio, but the remainder have more desirable physical properties associated with two-dimensional symmetry. The present case, which is modeled on a proposal made by the Princeton Plasma Physics Laboratory, has an $m = 2$ resonance with rotational transform $\iota = 0.5$ in each field period. It has been established that this has a bad effect on transport [8].

The Heliac geometry is not always easy to represent within the framework of a starlike limitation on the formula in the BETA code for the outermost flux surface. The best alternative is to express that flux surface by means of a trigonometric polynomial of low degree defined on the unit circle. This is accomplished using the option NGEOM = 5 in Subroutine SURF. The crescent of the Heliac is measured by the parameter DELC, which is the coefficient of the lead term in the polynomial. The input given below shows how to tune the code for convergence in a case like this with radical geometry and low aspect ratio.

To handle the Heliac geometry the coordinate system has been rotated as shown in the documentation for NGEOM = 5 in Section III.1. The input parameter IROT controls the rotation, and for Heliac cases IROT = 1. In order to improve the resolution for this complicated geometry more mesh points are taken in u and v than for cases like the ATF-1, so the crude grid for the Heliac is 7×18×18 instead of 7×12×12.

INPUT DATA AS READ FROM INPUT DATA DECK

EP	RBOU	QLZ	NRUN	NGEOM	RUN
0.3900	1.0000	3.0000	1	5	1000

DEL0	DEL1	DEL2	DEL3	DEL10	DEL20	DEL30
0.0000	1.0000	0.0100	0.0000	0.0000	0.0000	0.0000

DEL22	DEL33	DELA	DELB	DELC
0.2000	-0.0500	0.0500	1.0000	0.3800

XPR	YPR	ZPR	P0	AMU0	AMU1	AMU2
2.0000	1.5000	1.0000	0.1500	-0.5000	0.0000	-0.0300

ALF	ALFU
0.5000	-0.3000

NI	NJ	NK	ASYE	ERR
7	18	18	1.0E+03	1.0E-17

SA1	SA2	SA3	DT
4.1000	8.0000	0.5000	0.0150

SE1	SEMU	SEAX
600.00	0.50	4.00

SAFI	NE	NVAC
2.2000	100	-11

NR	NZ	NT	NAC	DPSI	GAM	IGAM
3	2	100	400	0.000	2.000	1

MIS	NIS	NAS	IROT	MF	NF	IPF
2	1	-5	1	4	3	4

IC	ITERF	TLIM
50	4000	500.0

PRINT1	PRINT2	PRINT3	PRINT4	PRINT5	PRINT6	PRINT7	PRINT8
AX ERR	RO ERR	PSI ERR	MU ERR	ROAX ERR	JAC RAT	DELENER	ENERGY

US0	UIN	USM	IVAX	BULGE	TILT	COIL
0.0000	0.0000	0.0000	0	0.0000	0.0000	0.0000

NIV	NV	NP	OM	SAFV	SE4	C1	C2
1	0	0	0.0000	0.0000	0.0000	0.0000	0.0000

KW1	KW2	AK3	TORS	AMPH	EVERT	WRAD	VERT
0	0	0.0000	0.0000	0.0000	0.0000	0.0000	0.0000

NRA1	NRA2	NZA1	NZA2	MK1	MK2	MK3	MK4
1	3	1	2	11	21	32	10

EL1	EL2	EM1	EM2	M	N
0.0000	0.0000	0.0000	0.0000	0	0

EAM1	EAM2	EAM3	EAM4	EAM5	EAM6
0.0000	0.0000	0.0000	0.0000	0.0000	0.0000

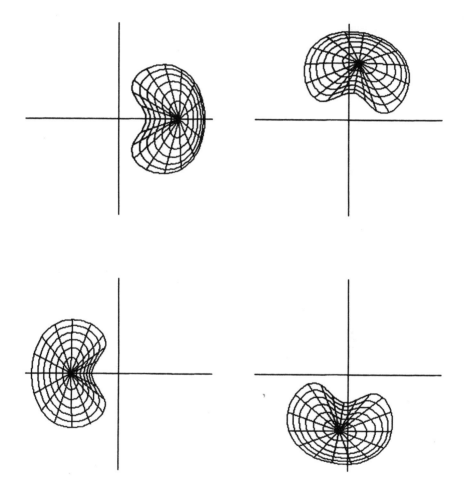

Fig. 11. Flux surfaces of a Heliac of low aspect ratio with moderate
bean shape specified by the parameter DELC = 0.38, and with ι = 0.5.

8. TJ-II Heliac equilibrium

The TJ-II is a Heliac experiment designed at the Oak Ridge National Laboratory for construction in Spain. There is considerable flexibility in the configuration. We have selected here a model in which the rotational transform ι lies in a desirable interval between 1/4 and 1/3 and has adequate shear. The equilibrium has been computed for $\beta = 0.05$ and has been used in extensive Monte Carlo studies of neoclassical transport for both ions and electrons (cf. Sections 13 and 14). The results seem to be quite promising for a successful experiment provided technical details can be attended to.

The cross sections of the TJ-II have a pronounced crescent shape that nearly violates the starlike requirement of the BETA code. Difficulties were experienced at the Oak Ridge National Laboratory in running this example. In the present run we have tuned the convergence parameters in a canonical fashion that may well be universally applicable to harder cases.

The Fourier coefficient DELC determines the amount of crescent. The geometry becomes quite eccentric for values of DELC larger than 0.4 and convergence becomes difficult. To improve the coordinate system we set ALF = 0.50 as discussed in Section 3, and NAC was put equal to 400 so that the acceleration scheme is not invoked until after the run has been launched. It should be noted that the magnetic axis must be initialized correctly, and the update for the initial values of RA and ZA for NGEOM = 5 is given in Section III.2.

INPUT DATA AS READ FROM INPUT DATA DECK

EP	RBOU	QLZ	NRUN	NGEOM	RUN	
0.1140	1.0000	4.0000	1	5	1000	

DEL0	DEL1	DEL2	DEL3	DEL10	DEL20	DEL30
0.0000	0.8400	0.0000	0.0000	0.0000	0.0000	0.0000

DEL22	DEL33	DELA	DELB	DELC	
0.3000	-0.0500	0.0000	1.0000	0.4000	

XPR	YPR	ZPR	P0	AMU0	AMU1	AMU2
1.0000	1.0000	1.0000	0.0520	-0.7000	0.0000	0.0100

ALF	ALFU	
0.5000	-0.5000	

NI	NJ	NK	ASYE	ERR
13	36	36	1.0E+03	1.0E-17

SA1	SA2	SA3	DT
4.0000	4.0000	0.5000	0.0100

SE1	SEMU	SEAX
600.00	0.50	4.00

SAFI	NE	NVAC
2.2000	100	-21

NR	NZ	NT	NAC	DPSI	GAM	IGAM
3	2	100	400	0.000	2.000	1

MIS	NIS	NAS	IROT	MF	NF	IPF
2	1	-5	1	6	3	7

IC	ITERF	TLIM
50	7200	3000.0

PRINT1	PRINT2	PRINT3	PRINT4	PRINT5	PRINT6	PRINT7	PRINT8
AX ERR	RO ERR	PSI ERR	MU ERR	ROAX ERR	JAC RAT	DELENER	ENERGY

USO	UIN	USM	IVAX	BULGE	TILT	COIL
0.0000	0.0000	0.0000	0	0.0000	0.0000	0.0000

NIV	NV	NP	OM	SAFV	SE4	C1	C2
1	0	0	0.0000	0.0000	0.0000	0.0000	0.0000

KW1	KW2	AK3	TORS	AMPH	EVERT	WRAD	VERT
0	0	0.0000	0.0000	0.0000	0.0000	0.0000	0.0000

NRA1	NRA2	NZA1	NZA2	MK1	MK2	MK3	MK4
1	3	1	2	11	21	32	10

EL1	EL2	EM1	EM2	M	N
0.0000	0.0000	0.0000	0.0000	0	0

EAM1	EAM0	EAM3	EAM4	EAM5	EAM6
0.0000	0.0000	0.0000	0.0000	0.0000	0.0000

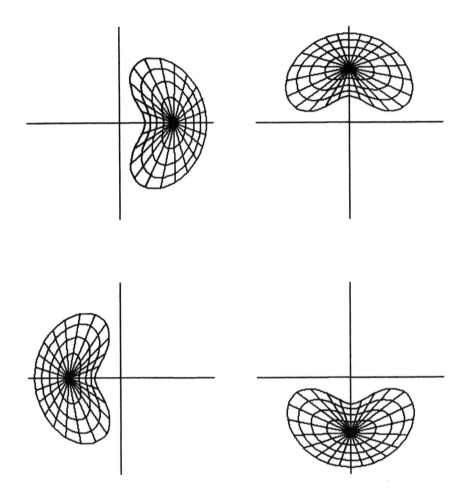

Fig. 12. Typical cross sections of the TJ-II Heliac designed at the Oak
Ridge National Laboratory for an experiment to be built in Spain.

9. Heliac stability for an m = 3 mode

The ideal form of a Heliac is a stellarator with two-dimensional helical symmetry. High β can be achieved in such a configuration, and the confinement time τ increases dramatically. For reactor applications it is desirable to maximize the product $\beta\tau$. There is both theoretical and numerical evidence that this scales like the cube of the major radius, R^3. Since a reactor has to be quite big anyway, it becomes reasonable to consider stellarators of very large aspect ratio so that at least the plasma radius can be relatively small.

The present example is a Heliac of aspect ratio 30 with 10 field periods and a rotational transform per field period that is close to $\iota = 0.3$. The run is drawn from a detailed study of the nonlinear m = 3 mode. Both the Mercier criterion and global stability calculations indicate that the β limit is at least 0.1. Our numerical work with the BETA code suggests more generally that any Heliac configuration with a substantial value of the crescent parameter DELC and an adequate helical excursion DEL1 has decisively better stability than most conventional stellarators. Our presentation concludes with a convergence study and a plot demonstrating the nonlinear stability of an m = 3 mode for A = 10, together with a graph of the confinement time.

The input file for this example exhibits a canonical tuning that works in most cases. Because an m = 3 mode is studied the input values EAM3 and EAM6 for the test function are different from zero, and DPSI = 0.02. This is actually an m = 3, n = 10 mode with NRUN = 1, and the test function is modified because of a rotation of coordinates when IROT = 1. To extrapolate to zero mesh size successfully we have used meshes finer than 13×36×36.

41

INPUT DATA AS READ FROM INPUT DATA DECK

EP	RBOU	QLZ	NRUN	NGEOM	RUN
0.0333	1.0000	10.0000	1	5	1000

DEL0	DEL1	DEL2	DEL3	DEL10	DEL20	DEL30
0.0000	1.0000	0.0000	0.0000	0.0000	0.0000	0.0000

DEL22	DEL33	DELA	DELB	DELC
0.2400	-0.0700	0.0400	1.0000	0.3800

XPR	YPR	ZPR	P0	AMU0	AMU1	AMU2
1.0000	1.0000	1.0000	0.1200	-0.7000	0.0000	-0.0300

ALF	ALFU
0.5000	-0.5000

NI	NJ	NK	ASYE	ERR
9	24	24	1.0E+03	1.0E-17

SA1	SA2	SA3	DT
4.0000	4.0000	0.5000	0.0150

SE1	SEMU	SEAX
600.00	0.50	4.00

SAFI	NE	NVAC
2.2000	100	-11

NR	NZ	NT	NAC	DPSI	GAM	IGAM
3	2	-4200	400	0.020	2.000	1

MIS	NIS	NAS	IROT	MF	NF	IPF
2	1	-5	1	6	3	4

IC	ITERF	TLIM
50	7200	3000.0

PRINT1	PRINT2	PRINT3	PRINT4	PRINT5	PRINT6	PRINT7	PRINT8
AX ERR	RO ERR	PSI ERR	MU ERR	ROAX ERR	JAC RAT	DELENER	ENERGY

US0	UIN	USM	IVAX	BULGE	TILT	COIL
0.0000	0.0000	0.0000	0	0.0000	0.0000	0.0000

NIV	NV	NP	OM	SAFV	SE4	C1	C2
1	0	0	0.0000	0.0000	0.0000	0.0000	0.0000

KW1	KW2	AK3	TORS	AMPH	EVERT	WRAD	VERT
0	0	0.0000	0.0000	0.0000	0.0000	0.0000	0.0000

NRA1	NRA2	NZA1	NZA2	MK1	MK2	MK3	MK4
1	3	1	2	11	21	32	10

EL1	EL2	EM1	EM2	M	N
0.0000	0.0000	0.0000	0.0000	3	1

EAM1	EAM2	EAM3	EAM4	EAM5	EAM6
0.0000	0.0000	2.0000	0.0000	0.0000	-1.0000

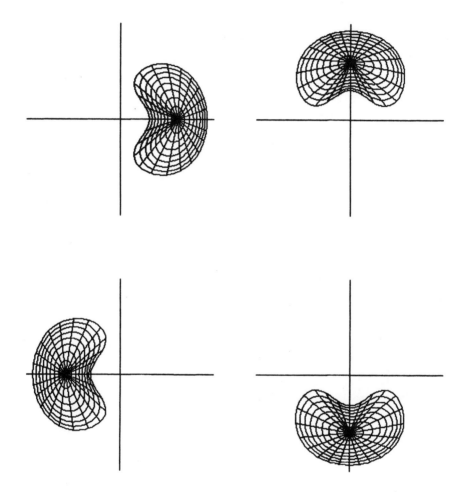

Fig. 13. Flux surfaces of a Heliac with 10 field periods and aspect ratio 30 that has been optimized for performance as a reactor.

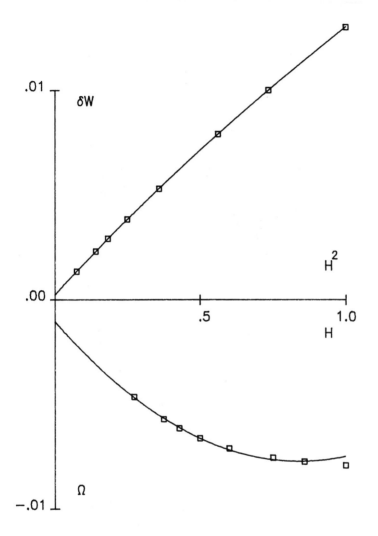

Fig. 14. Convergence study of nonlinear and local stability. Least squares extrapolation to zero mesh size h is shown for the m = 3 energy variation δW and the Mercier criterion Ω of a Heliac with EP = 0.1, QLZ = 6, DEL1 = 0.6, DELC = 0.38, and p = 0.06(1-s). The value h = 1 corresponds to 6×18×18 mesh cells. A cubic polynomial of the form $A_0 + A_2h^2 + A_3h^3$ is used to fit the data for δW, but a quadratic polynomial $A_0 + A_1h + A_2h^2$ is used to fit the data for Ω.

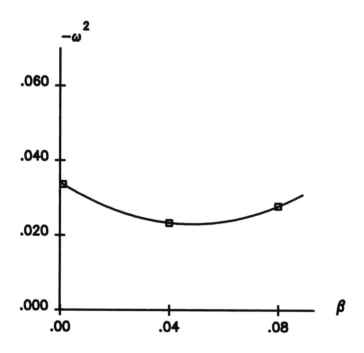

Fig. 15. Nonlinear stability of a Heliac with six field periods. The m = 3, n = 6 mode is shown with EP = 0.1, QLZ = 6, DEL1 = 0.6, DEL22 = 0.24, DELB = 1.0, DELC = 0.38, and $1.5 < \iota < 2.0$.

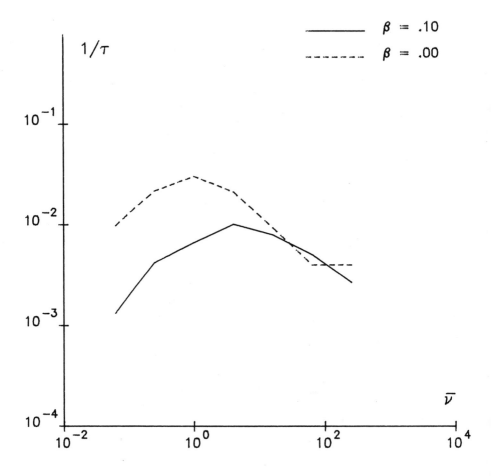

Fig. 16. Dependence of confinement time on β. Reciprocal ion confinement times τ are plotted for a Heliac with EP = 0.033, QLZ = 10, and ρ_L= 0.01 at two values of β.

10.   Heliac free boundary equilibrium

To illustrate the use of the sharp boundary option in the BETA code we present a free boundary Heliac equilibrium. The winding law is specified by means of a Dirichlet boundary condition on the scalar potential of the magnetic field which is imposed at an outer control surface. If the potential were calculated outside that surface by solving a Neumann problem, one might estimate the shape of the coils necessary to produce the equilibrium by examining the jump in the tangential derivative of that potential, which is related to the surface current. Without such a calculation our representation of the boundary values of the potential merely gives a qualitative description of the winding law (cf. Section 6). This is determined by formulas involving the input parameters WRAD, BULGE,... given on Cards 28, 30 and 32 of the input file.

We have studied modular winding laws that might serve to construct in a practical fashion a Heliac configuration such as we display here [4]. Our run serves as an indication of existence of the desired equilibrium. However, because of incompatibilities in the formulation of the problem the existence is established only in the asymptotic sense that there is an acceptable answer for a suitably small but positive value of the mesh size. The behavior of magnetic surfaces improves in the two-dimensional limit of large aspect ratio. Numerical experimentation shows that as β increases there is little change in the rotational transform, the location of the magnetic axis, or the shape of the separatrix. However, it should also be observed that for a Heliac there are many harmonics present in the equilibrium even at $\beta = 0$.

INPUT DATA AS READ FROM INPUT DATA DECK

EP	RBOU	QLZ	NRUN	NGEOM	RUN
0.0700	0.4500	10.0000	1	5	1000

DEL0	DEL1	DEL2	DEL3	DEL10	DEL20	DEL30
0.0000	0.4500	0.0000	0.0000	0.0000	0.0000	0.0000

DEL22	DEL33	DELA	DELB	DELC
0.1000	0.0000	0.0000	1.0000	0.3500

XPR	YPR	ZPR	PO	AMU0	AMU1	AMU2
1.0000	1.0000	1.0000	0.1300	-0.7000	0.0000	0.0100

ALF	ALFU
0.0000	-0.3500

NI	NJ	NK	ASYE	ERR
9	24	24	1.0E+03	1.0E-17

SA1	SA2	SA3	DT
4.0000	8.0000	0.5000	0.0075

SE1	SEMU	SEAX
300.00	0.20	-2.00

SAFI	NE	NVAC
2.2000	100	21

NR	NZ	NT	NAC	DPSI	GAM	IGAM
3	2	100	200	0.000	2.000	1

MIS	NIS	NAS	IROT	MF	NF	IPF
1	1	-5	1	6	3	4

IC	ITERF	TLIM
50	5000	1000.0

PRINT1	PRINT2	PRINT3	PRINT4	PRINT5	PRINT6	PRINT7	PRINT8
AX ERR	RO ERR	PSI ERR	VAC ERR	OAX ERR	JAC RAT	MU ERR	BOU ERR

USO	UIN	USM	IVAX	BULGE	TILT	COIL
0.5000	0.0000	-1.0000	1	0.1200	0.0500	0.1000

NIV	NV	NP	OM	SAFV	SE4	C1	C2
9	3	1	1.6800	2.0000	1.0000	0.0000	11.0000

KW1	KW2	AK3	TORS	AMPH	EVERT	WRAD	VERT
1	0	1.0000	0.0000	-0.7000	-1.0000	1.5000	0.0000

NRA1	NRA2	NZA1	NZA2	MK1	MK2	MK3	MK4
1	3	1	2	11	21	31	10

EL1	EL2	EM1	EM2	M	N
0.0000	0.0000	0.0000	0.0000	0	0

EAM1	EAM2	EAM3	EAM4	EAM5	EAM6
0.0000	0.0000	0.0000	0.0000	0.0000	0.0000

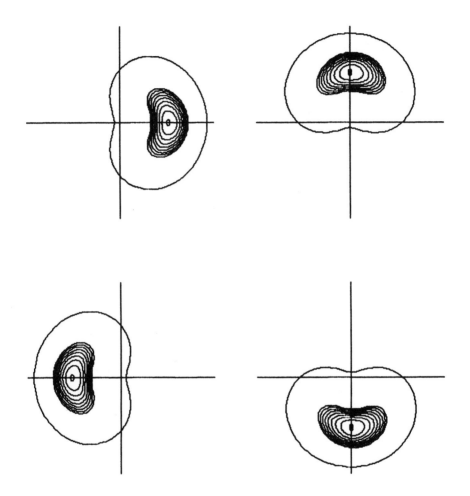

Fig. 17. Free boundary calculation of equilibrium establishing that the rotational transform and flux surfaces of an optimized Heliac configuration change little with β for a fixed choice of the winding law.

11. Helias nonlinear stability test

The Helias is a stellarator with multiple harmonics designed by Nuehrenberg and Zille [26] at the Max Planck Institute for Plasma Physics in Garching to maximize β while keeping the rotational transform under unity. Extensive runs of the BETA code were used to find an optimal choice of parameters based on the Mercier local stability criterion. The resulting configuration turns out to be a major improvement on the Heliac for aspect ratio A = 11.5. At β = 0.05 the Mercier quantity Ω remains above zero and the geometric confinement time is over 200.

To verify the nonlinear stability of the Helias we have applied a test of the m = 1 mode like those described for the Wendelstein VII-AS and the ATF-1. NRUN was chosen so that the total rotational transform ι for all NRUN periods is approximately unity at the outer wall and becomes compatible with the test function we use to study stability. Thus we have used eight field periods rather than the five of the actual configuration to establish global stability for β = 0.05. The present run is drawn from a series for this calculation that used meshes of up to 13×24×48×8 points and took 10 hours on the Cray 2 computer. The result seems to confirm a contention that success for the Mercier criterion $\Omega \geq 0$ is likely to imply nonlinear stability.

The Helias makes use of a more elaborate set of harmonics than is available through a conventional choice of the parameter NGEOM in Subroutine SURF. What is therefore required is to code independently the appropriate formulas for r and z and their first derivatives with respect to u and v. Fig. 18 displays the unusual cross sections for equilibrium, and Fig. 19 shows an analysis of transport. Like the Wendelstein VII-AS the geometry for this case is best input using NGEOM = 4, but that option must be updated as follows:

In the CLICHE statements at the beginning NAME16 becomes

```
CLICHE NAME16
COMMON /GABO/ DEL1R,DEL1Z,DEL(5,5)
ENDCLICHE
```

In the main routine the first five lines after Statement 10 are replaced

by

```
READ(25,1680) DEL1R,DEL1Z,DEL(4,3),DEL(1,3),DEL(2,3),
1 DEL(4,4),DEL(1,2)
READ(25,1720)
READ (25,1680) DEL(3,2),DEL(5,4),DEL(5,5),DEL(3,3),DEL(1,4),
1 DEL(2,4),DEL(3,4)
```

The four lines after Statement 50 are replaced by

```
PRINT 1760, DEL1R,DEL1Z,DEL(4,3),DEL(1,3),DEL(2,3),DEL(4,4),
1 DEL(1,2)
PRINT 1770, DEL(3,2),DEL(5,4),DEL(5,5),DEL(3,3),DEL(1,4),
1 DEL(2,4),DEL(3,4)
```

FORMAT Statements 1500 and 1760 are replaced by

```
1500 FORMAT(13X,3HUSO,5X,3HUIN,5X,3HUSM,4X,4HIVAX,5X,
1 3HC32,5X,3HC21,5X,3HC20/8X,3F8.4,3X,I5,3F8.4//)
1760 FORMAT(11X,5HDEL1R,3X,5HDEL1Z,3X,5HDEL20,2X,6HDEL-10,3X,
1 5HDEL40,3X,5HDEL21,1X,7HDEL-1-1/9X,7(F7.4,1X)//)
```

In Subroutine SURF the 11th through 14th lines of code after Statement

90 are replaced by

```
DO 100 LL=1,5
DO 100 MM=1,5
L=LL-3
M=MM-2
XX1=COS(L*UBAR-(M-1)*VP1)*DEL(LL,MM)
XX2=SIN(L*UBAR-(M-1)*VP1)*DEL(LL,MM)
```

The BETA codes have been used to design a variety of stellarators with multiple harmonics that have desirable properties, such as providing direct access to the second stability region [4]. We can take advantage of the knowledge about multiple harmonics to define a configuration that does not represent a major departure from the established Heliotron E and ATF-1 experiments, yet offers the prospect of achieving higher β and better confinement. To this end the basic $\ell = 2$ coil is modulated to generate a large sideband to which we ascribe the $\ell = -1$ label because of conventions adopted in the NGEOM = 5 option. The essential features of the Helias are retained, but most of the complication is gone. A free boundary run of this $\ell = -1,2$ stellarator

51

can be used to specify its winding law. For that purpose we represent the boundary values of the scalar potential ϕ = PT in Subroutine PBOU by the formula

$$PT = C2*V + VERT*Z + AMPH*WRAD*ATAN(SIN(2U-V)/(WRAD-COS(2U-V)))$$

on a control surface swept out by a rotating ellipse with a helical excursion.

Difficulties are encountered in constructing a similar winding law for the Helias itself because so many small harmonics occur that are sensitive to change, and because prescribing the shape of the free boundary is not a well posed problem. However, the simple winding law modeled by the formula we have given consists of two coils like those of the Heliotron E with a vertical field included. Modulation specified by the parameter TORS can be used to introduce additional helical excursion of the magnetic axis. The plasma may be expected to exhibit the desirable magnetic surfaces shown in Fig. 20 if the coils have appropriate rectangular cross sections that are placed at right angles and rotate through 90° in one field period. For odd QLZ the main coil might consist of a single filament defined by the formula

$$r + iz = \sum_{n=1,2,4} R_n \, e^{iv/n} \; .$$

Interesting fixed boundary versions of the ℓ = -1,2 stellarator are run by putting NGEOM = 5, IROT = 1, AMU0 = -0.9, ALFU = -0.5, EP = 0.11, and DELB = 1. Then with QLZ = 8, DEL2 = DELC = 0.3, and all the remaining parameters on Cards 4 and 6 set equal to zero we obtain a case with minimal helical excursion of the magnetic axis and with $0.70 < \iota < 0.95$. Nonlinear stability tests of the resonant $m = n = 1$ and $m = n = 2$ modes suggest that the β limit exceeds 5%, for a positive helical excursion shifts the stability curves safely to the right. A similar

52

example with QLZ = 7, DEL1 = DEL2 = DELC = 0.34 and DEL22 = 0.05, DELA = 0.02 has $1.1 < \iota < 1.4$ at $\beta = 0.03$, and it is flux conserving in the sense that ι does not vary significantly as β increases. More shear is obtained by putting QLZ = 8, DEL1 = DEL2 = DELC = 0.3 and DEL33 = -0.1 instead so that ι covers the range $1.1 < \iota < 1.9$. Both of the latter cases ought to be stable because the level of the parallel current remains exceptionally low. A magnetic hill $V''/V' > 0$ comparable to that of the Heliotron E is present, but the $\ell = -1,2$ stellarator has a much bigger geometric confinement time $r > 120$.

The $\ell = -1,2$ stellarator couples a standard $\ell = 2$ coil to harmonics like those of the Heliac possessing two-dimensional symmetry when EP = 0. Like the Helias it is designed to reduce the parallel current $\lambda = J \cdot B/p'B^2$. This both improves the Mercier criterion and reduces transport, but correspondingly introduces a magnetic hill that may however be harmless in view of experience with the Heliotron E. The Mercier criterion suggests more generally that safe access to the second stability region may never be achieved because instabilities will appear in higher ideal or resistive modes. A similar phenomenon occurred in our inner tube analysis of nonlinear stability for the Heliotron E in Section 3, which implies that increasing the aspect ratio does not stabilize all the higher modes. However, even after higher modes have become unstable a laboratory plasma may continue to be confined in a regime characterized by a soft β limit associated with deterioration of the magnetic surfaces. In this connection poor behavior at the magnetic axis can be analyzed by inner tube runs of the equilibrium code with very small values of EP. Assuming that the harmonics with $\ell \geq 3$ have become negligible, we are led to the problem of optimizing a configuration of large aspect ratio with only the coefficients Δ_{1n} and Δ_{2n} different from zero. The conclusion from such a study seems to be that some helical excursion of the magnetic axis is necessary for good confinement at large β.

INPUT DATA AS READ FROM INPUT DATA DECK

EP	RBOU	QLZ	NRUN	NGEOM	RUN
0.0870	1.0000	5.0000	8	4	1003

DEL1R	DEL1Z	DEL20	DEL-10	DEL40	DEL21	DEL-1-1
0.8000	0.4000	0.1000	-0.0500	0.0000	0.2900	-0.2400

DEL41	DEL22	DEL32	DEL42	DEL23	DEL33	DEL43
0.0000	0.0000	-0.0700	0.0000	0.0000	0.0000	0.0000

DEL0	ALFU2	ALFU3
0.0700	0.0000	0.0000

XPR	YPR	ZPR	P0	AMU0	AMU1	AMU2
1.0000	1.0000	1.0000	0.0300	0.1000	0.0000	0.0000

ALF	ALFU
0.5000	-0.5000

NI	NJ	NK	ASYE	ERR
13	24	48	1.0E+03	1.0E-19

SA1	SA2	SA3	DT
4.0000	4.0000	0.5000	0.0065

SE1	SEMU	SEAX
600.00	0.50	4.00

SAFI	NE	NVAC
2.2000	100	-11

NR	NZ	NT	NAC	DPSI	GAM	IGAM
3	2	-13800	400	0.100	2.000	1

MIS	NIS	NAS	IROT	MF	NF	IPF
1	0	-5	0	6	4	7

IC	ITERF	TLIM
50	26000	36000.0

PRINT1	PRINT2	PRINT3	PRINT4	PRINT5	PRINT6	PRINT7	PRINT8
AX ERR	RO ERR	PSI ERR	FPSI	ROAX ERR	JAC RAT	DELENER	ENERGY

USO	UIN	USM	IVAX	BULGE	TILT	COIL
0.0000	0.0000	0.0000	0	0.0000	0.0000	0.0000

NIV	NV	NP	OM	SAFV	SE4	C1	C2
1	0	0	0.0000	0.0000	0.0000	0.0000	0.0000

KW1	KW2	AK3	TORS	AMPH	EVERT	WRAD	VERT
0	0	0.0000	0.0000	0.0000	0.0000	0.0000	0.0000

NRA1	NRA2	NZA1	NZA2	MK1	MK2	MK3	MK4
1	3	1	2	11	21	31	10

EL1	EL2	EM1	EM2	M	N
1.0000	0.0000	1.0000	0.0000	1	1

EAM1	EAM2	EAM3	EAM4	EAM5	EAM6
2.0000	0.0000	0.0000	-1.0000	0.0000	0.0000

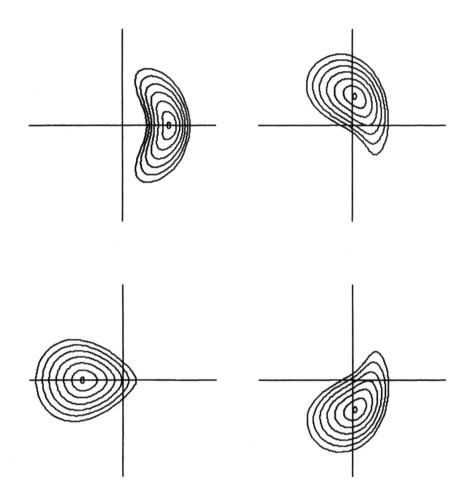

Fig. 18. The Helias equilibrium designed at the Max Planck Institute for Plasma Physics in Garching to satisfy the Mercier stability criterion when $\beta = 0.05$.

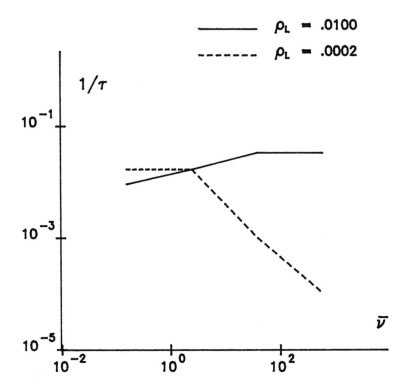

Fig. 19. Dependence of ion and electron loss rates on the collision frequency for Helias. Reciprocal ion and electron confinement times are plotted at comparable collision frequencies with A = 11.5, β = 0.03, and 0.5 < ι < 0.7 .

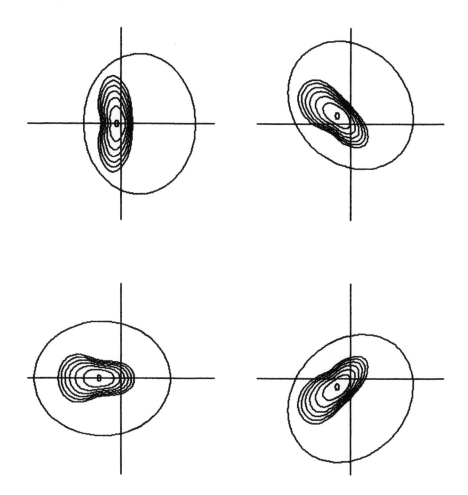

Fig. 20. Winding law for an $\ell = -1,2$ stellarator found by modifying the run in Section 6 so that EP = 0.25, QLZ = 7, DEL1 = 0.3, DEL2 = 0.1, P0 = 0.05, ALFU = 0, SA2 = 16., IVAX = 1, C2 = 3.6, TORS = 0.5, AMPH = - 0.35, WRAD = 1.1, VERT = -0.05 and BULGE = TILT = COIL = 0.

12. Bifurcated tokamak equilibrium

For a tokamak run of the BETA code one fixes the rotational transform by setting NVAC < 10, in contrast with stellarator cases where one iterates on the rotational transform to reduce the net current to zero. The present run describes a bifurcated tokamak equilibrium in which the helical excursion of the magnetic axis is held at a value different from zero by setting NT = ITERF and initializing r and z in the code appropriately. This three-dimensional equilibrium might be interpreted as a simulation of the transient effects of magnetohydrodynamic activity on a tokamak. We have inserted it into our Monte Carlo transport code to estimate ion and electron confinement times τ_i and τ_e. Because of the infinite width of the banana orbits in any truly three-dimensional configuration, τ_i and τ_e become equal at low collision frequencies, as we show in a plot for the present example. The BETA codes are applicable to tokamaks, but only become worthwhile in cases where three-dimensional effects are significant.

To perform an axially symmetric, two-dimensional run one sets ASYE = 10^{-8}, and the computer time is considerably reduced. However, this example is three-dimensional because we have initialized the helical excursion of the magnetic axis at the value $\Delta_1 = 0.1$ by replacing the two instructions after Statement 50 in Subroutine SURF by

```
RA(K)=0.1*X3=0.1*COS(VP1)
ZA(K)=0.1*X2=0.1*SIN(VP1)
```

INPUT DATA AS READ FROM INPUT DATA DECK

EP	RBOU	QLZ	NRUN	NGEOM	RUN
0.3333	1.0000	1.0000	1	1	1010

DEL0	DEL1	DEL2	DEL3	DEL10	DEL20	DEL30
0.0000	0.0000	0.0000	0.0000	0.0000	0.0000	0.0000

DEL22	DEL33	DELA	DELB	DELC
0.0000	0.0000	0.0000	0.0000	0.0000

XPR	YPR	ZPR	P0	AMU0	AMU1	AMU2
1.0000	1.0000	1.0000	0.0300	1.0500	0.0000	-0.7500

ALF	ALFU
0.5000	0.0000

NI	NJ	NK	ASYE	ERR
13	24	24	1.0E-05	1.0E-17

SA1	SA2	SA3	DT
4.0000	4.0000	0.5000	0.0150

SE1	SEMU	SEAX
600.00	0.50	4.00

SAFI	NE	NVAC
2.2000	100	-1

NR	NZ	NT	NAC	DPSI	GAM	IGAM
3	2	5000	400	0.000	2.000	1

MIS	NIS	NAS	IROT	MF	NF	IPF
2	1	-5	0	6	4	7

IC	ITERF	TLIM
50	5000	1000.0

PRINT1	PRINT2	PRINT3	PRINT4	PRINT5	PRINT6	PRINT7	PRINT8
AX ERR	RO ERR	PSI ERR	MU ERR	ROAX ERR	JAC RAT	DELENER	ENERGY

US0	UIN	USM	IVAX	BULGE	TILT	COIL
0.0000	0.0000	0.0000	0	0.0000	0.0000	0.0000

NIV	NV	NP	OM	SAFV	SE4	C1	C2
1	0	0	0.0000	0.0000	0.0000	0.0000	0.0000

KW1	KW2	AK3	TORS	AMPH	EVERT	WRAD	VERT
0	0	0.0000	0.0000	0.0000	0.0000	0.0000	0.0000

NRA1	NRA2	NZA1	NZA2	MK1	MK2	MK3	MK4
1	3	1	2	11	21	32	10

EL1	EL2	EM1	EM2	M	N
0.0000	0.0000	0.0000	0.0000	0	0

EAM1	EAM2	EAM3	EAM4	EAM5	EAM6
0.0000	0.0000	0.0000	0.0000	0.0000	0.0000

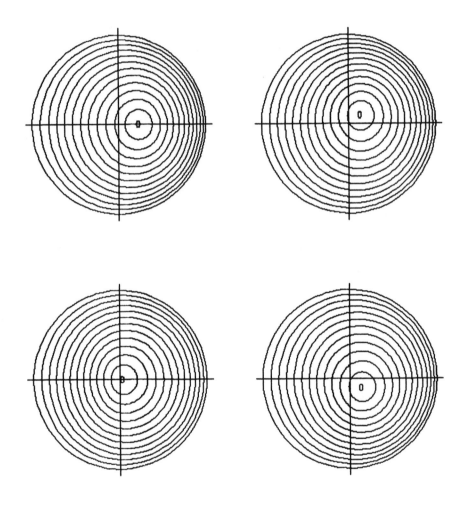

Fig. 21. Bifurcated tokamak equilibrium exhibiting helical excursion of the magnetic axis.

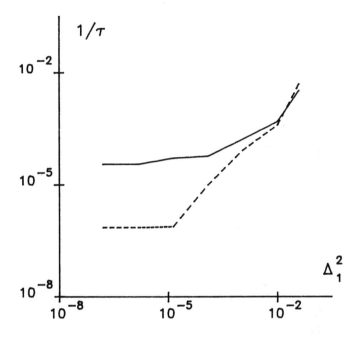

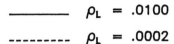

$\rho_L = .0100$

$\rho_L = .0002$

Fig. 22. Dependence of confinement time in the bifurcated tokamak on three-dimensional effects that model nonlinear instabilities. Reciprocal ion and electron confinement times are plotted versus the helical excursion Δ_1 of the magnetic axis for equilibria with $0.4 < \iota < 1.1$, EP $= 0.33$ and $\beta = 0.001$ at collision frequency $\bar{\nu} = 0.25$.

P_{00}	P_{11}	P_{32}	τ_i	τ_e	C_{11}	C_{32}
-.5	0.000	0.000	7000	7000	0.03	-.02
0.0	0.000	0.000	700	1000	0.02	0.05
0.0	-.003	0.000	500	1300	-.10	0.00
0.0	0.000	-.003	500	1100	-.08	0.02
0.0	0.003	-.003	500	700	-.11	-.05
0.0	0.010	0.000	300	100	-.20	0.00

Table 1. Fourier coefficients C_{mn} of the charge separation

$$\langle F_i \rangle - \langle F_e \rangle = \Sigma\ C_{mn}\cos(m\tilde{\psi}-n\tilde{\phi})$$

versus Fourier coefficients P_{mn} of the electric potential

$$\Phi = P_{00}(1-s) + \Sigma\ P_{mn}\ \cos(m\tilde{\psi}-n\tilde{\phi})$$

for the bifurcated tokamak with dimensionless collision frequency $\bar{\nu} = 1/4$ and with gyroradii $\rho_i = 0.01$ for ions and $\rho_e = 0.0002$ for electrons. The calculation is inadequate to determine roots of the quasineutrality equations $C_{mn} = 0$ at this low collision frequency, but the effect of a resonant electric field becomes evident in the last row of data.

13. Calculation of ion confinement time

Here we present a run of the Monte Carlo code written to compute neoclassical transport of ions or electrons from the equilibrium data listed on Tapes 2 and 7 of the equilibrium code (cf. Ch. IV). A drift kinetic equation is solved by a method of split time which alternates between an orbit solver and a random walk modeling the collision operator. Besides Tapes 2 and 7, the principal input parameters are a dimensionless collision frequency FREQ which is approximately 1 for reactors and a gyroradius RADL which is represented in units of the plasma radius. Confinement times and loss rates are estimated from the exponential decay of the distribution function. The confinement time is output in units that reduce to milliseconds when the average toroidal field is 1 tesla. Tapes 2 and 7 for this example were obtained from the TJ-II Heliac fixed boundary equilibrium listed in Section 8.

To calculate transport it suffices in most cases to compute the equilibrium on a mesh of 13×24×24 points. What is required from the equilibrium is a Fourier series for $1/B^2$ which is adequately approximated by 20 or 30 terms in most cases. First the Fourier series is truncated at the poloidal and toroidal indices MF and NF, but afterward only terms whose norms are bigger than the prescribed value SIZEL are retained. Typically we follow 256 orbits for time TEND = 1, which may take an hour on the Cray 1. The electric potential is input at will through the parameters E0, E1, E2, and E3 in Subroutine ELPOT. One can either put it equal to zero or attempt to determine it from quasineutrality equations by a spectral method. For this example we have chosen it so that the ion confinement time τ_i nearly coincides with the electron confinement time τ_e, which is the one to be found in Section 14. The next four pages display typical printed output whose significance is described in Section IV.2. Fig. 23 is a plot by the code to assess exponential decay of the distribution function, and Figs. 24 and 25 display sample histograms that are output.

INPUT

NS	NPSI	NPHI	NMAG	NEK	NTE1	NTE2	TE1
4	4	4	2	2	1	1	0.9900

FREQ	FREQE	DELT	TEND	SEED	SIZEL	NPOL	NCOL
64.0000	64.0000	0.0100	1.0000	644.00	0.0080	2	1

RADL	E0	E1	E2	E3	ACC	MF	NF
0.01000	-1.5000	0.0000	0.0000	-0.0200	5.0000	4	3

IC	NPRT	TLIM	NRUN	NSTU	NOFC		TITLE
20	-1	2000.0	300	0	6		TJ-II

FOURIER COEFFICIENTS OF DISTRIBUTION FUNCTION

M	N	K
0	1	0
1	-1	1
1	0	1
10	-7	0
3	-2	0
17	-12	0

DATA USED FROM EQUILIBRIUM RUN

EP	RBOU	QLZ	RUN
0.1140	1.0000	4.0000	1000

NI	NJ	NK	NIV	NVAC
13	36	36	0	-21

MF	NF	IROT	C1	C2
9	4	1	0.0000	0.0000

BO = 1.012   AVERAGE PLASMA RADIUS = 1.119

	C(M-N)	C(M+N)	S(M+N)	S(M-N)
NUMBER OF FOURIER TERMS REPRESENTING MAGNETIC FIELD	7	8	0	0

FOURIER COEFFICIENTS OF 1/B*B

COS(M PSI - N PHI)

J	M	N	NORM	1	S	S**2
1	0	0	5.277E-01	0.559	-0.060	-0.018
2	1	0	8.831E-02	0.156	-0.042	0.000
3	1	1	8.300E-02	-0.163	0.068	0.000
4	0	1	3.817E-02	0.060	-0.048	-0.009
5	2	0	2.271E-02	-0.059	0.022	0.000
6	2	1	1.718E-02	0.050	-0.025	0.000
7	1	2	8.798E-03	0.018	-0.008	0.000
8	3	0	5.057E-03	0.011	0.000	0.000
9	0	2	4.837E-03	-0.007	0.002	0.006
10	3	1	3.877E-03	-0.006	0.000	0.000
11	4	1	2.313E-03	0.004	0.000	0.000
12	4	0	2.234E-03	-0.006	0.000	0.000
13	2	2	9.896E-04	-0.001	-0.001	0.000
14	1	3	8.436E-04	-0.001	0.000	0.000
15	3	2	7.372E-04	-0.002	0.000	0.000
16	0	3	4.725E-04	0.000	0.001	-0.001
17	4	2	4.642E-04	0.001	0.000	0.000
18	3	3	2.479E-04	0.001	0.000	0.000
19	2	3	1.715E-04	-0.001	0.002	0.000
20	4	3	1.318E-04	0.000	0.000	0.000

COS(M PSI + N PHI)

J	M	N	NORM	1	S	S**2
1	0	0	5.277E-01	0.559	-0.060	-0.018
2	1	1	1.614E-01	0.287	-0.080	0.000
3	1	0	8.831E-02	0.156	-0.042	0.000
4	0	1	3.817E-02	0.060	-0.048	-0.009
5	2	1	3.607E-02	0.069	0.001	0.000
6	2	0	2.271E-02	-0.059	0.022	0.000
7	2	2	1.858E-02	0.037	-0.001	0.000
8	3	2	8.290E-03	0.020	0.000	0.000
9	3	0	5.057E-03	0.011	0.000	0.000
10	3	1	4.926E-03	-0.011	0.000	0.000
11	0	2	4.837E-03	-0.007	0.002	0.006
12	3	3	2.718E-03	0.007	0.000	0.000
13	4	0	2.234E-03	-0.006	0.000	0.000
14	4	3	2.029E-03	0.006	0.000	0.000
15	4	1	1.625E-03	0.004	0.000	0.000
16	1	2	1.339E-03	0.006	-0.009	0.000
17	1	3	5.140E-04	-0.002	0.002	0.000
18	0	3	4.725E-04	0.000	0.001	-0.001
19	4	2	4.298E-04	0.001	0.000	0.000
20	2	3	2.592E-04	0.000	0.000	0.000

FOURIER COEFFICIENTS OF DISTRIBUTION FUNCTION

(S**K/2)*COS(M*PSI-N*PHI)

TIME	0,1,0	1,-1,1	1,0,1	10,-7,0	3,-2,0	17,-12,0
0.104	0.078	0.102	0.190	0.040	0.129	-.064
0.110	0.048	0.067	0.151	-.001	0.068	-.015
0.115	0.023	0.108	0.145	0.005	0.054	-.011
0.120	0.039	0.117	0.148	-.003	0.024	-.007
0.125	0.046	0.118	0.151	0.002	0.032	-.008
0.130	0.051	0.116	0.138	0.001	0.014	-.006
0.136	0.052	0.124	0.131	0.004	0.014	-.007
0.141	0.057	0.134	0.138	0.002	0.015	-.005
0.146	0.061	0.140	0.139	0.002	0.013	-.007
0.151	0.058	0.135	0.141	0.003	0.008	-.005
0.157	0.053	0.121	0.141	0.000	0.012	-.004
0.162	0.055	0.124	0.141	0.002	0.010	-.006
0.167	0.062	0.124	0.141	0.001	0.010	-.005
0.172	0.064	0.126	0.137	0.002	0.007	-.005
0.177	0.065	0.123	0.136	0.001	0.002	-.003
0.183	0.067	0.125	0.134	0.001	0.008	-.003
0.188	0.069	0.130	0.134	0.001	0.005	-.003
0.193	0.067	0.128	0.134	0.002	0.006	-.003
0.198	0.067	0.125	0.134	0.001	0.003	-.003
0.203	0.066	0.124	0.132	0.002	0.005	-.003
0.209	0.069	0.124	0.134	0.000	0.004	-.003

FINAL RADL = 0.01052

OUTPUT

NUMBER LOST =   0   NUMBER REMAINING =   256

COLLISION TIME =   0.26   PERIODS TRAVERSED =   198.9

ENERCON =   3.194E-06   CPU TIME =   1251 S

MEAN FREE PATH / FIELD PERIOD =   27.6

CONFINEMENT TIME TAU AND LOSS RATE   1/TAU

CONFINEMENT TIME = 72   EQUIVALENT TO   72 MS AT 1 TESLA

1-S TEST FUNCTION

	TIME INTERVAL	TAU	LOSS RATE	STANDARD DEVIATION
FULL INTERVAL	1.88	46.2	0.022	0.012
HALF INTERVAL	0.94	63.8	0.016	0.013

COSINE TEST FUNCTION

	TIME INTERVAL	TAU	LOSS RATE	STANDARD DEVIATION
FULL INTERVAL	1.88	63.0	0.016	0.003
HALF INTERVAL	0.94	72.0	0.014	0.004

PARTICLE LOSS TEST FUNCTION

	TIME INTERVAL	TAU	LOSS RATE	STANDARD DEVIATION
FULL INTERVAL	1.88	**********	0.000	0.000
HALF INTERVAL	0.94	**********	0.000	0.000

EXPONENTIAL DECAY OF EXPECTED VALUES

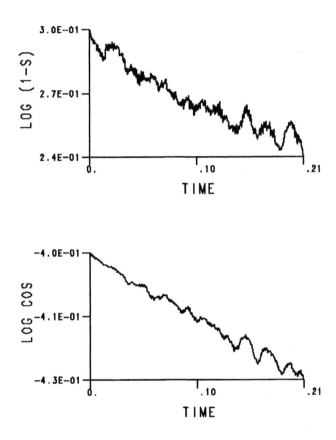

Fig. 23. Plots output by the transport code to assess exponential decay of expected values of integrals of the distribution function. The first graph exhibits the decay of (1-s), and the second one shows the decay of the cosine function Γ specified in Section IV.1.

HISTOGRAMS

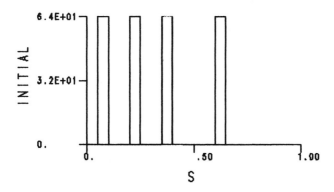

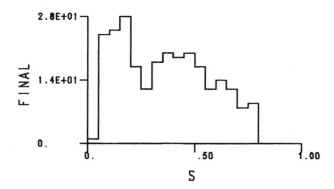

Fig. 24. Histograms output by the transport code to display properties of the distribution function. Initial and final distributions of the toroidal flux s are shown.

HISTOGRAMS

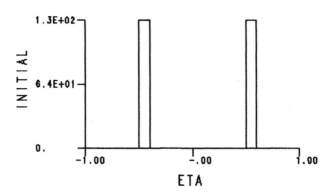

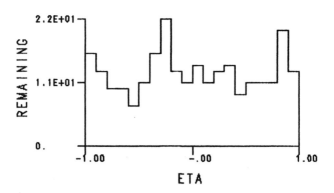

Fig. 25. Histograms output by the transport code to display properties of the distribution function. Initial and final distributions of the velocity parameter $\eta = v_{\parallel}/v$ are plotted.

14. Calculation of electron confinement time

For high collision frequencies the Monte Carlo value of the electron confinement time with no electric field exceeds the corresponding value of the ion confinement time by a factor equal to the square root of the mass ratio. The charge neutrality condition imposed by Coulomb's law suggests that not only should these times be equal, but also the distribution functions for ions and electrons should agree to several significant figures. In the Monte Carlo code we calculate the Fourier coefficients of the distribution function by estimating expected values of the appropriate trigonometric functions. Quasineutrality equations asserting that the Fourier coefficients of the charge separation vanish can be solved numerically to determine the Fourier coefficients of the electric potential. For low collision frequencies this turns out to be feasible in practice because the matrix relating the two arrays of coefficients is more or less diagonally dominant.

In the present run the electric field has been selected so that the electron confinement time is nearly equal to the ion confinement time for the corresponding case specified in our previous example. For this electron run RADL is input as a negative number -0.0002 which is 50 times smaller than the gyroradius RADL = 0.01 for the comparable ion run. The code renormalizes so that the collision frequencies are similarly in a ratio of 64, although the input values are identical. The electron confinement time is estimated from the expected value of a carefully constructed cosine function (cf. Section IV.1) because of the necessarily short duration of the run in physical time. The results for the confinement time and the Fourier coefficients have only one significant figure. For higher collision frequencies the Fourier coefficients of the charge separation become so small that they lose their significance, and Ohm's law is recovered for the determination of the electric potential Φ. This is because of a reduction in the length scale between collisions. However, very small resonant terms in Φ which

71

vary little along the magnetic lines of force are still found to have a decisive effect that may bring the electron confinement time into line with the ion confinement time. The present example is drawn from the TJ-II Heliac equilibrium given in Section 8, which makes the resonance phenomenon easier to discern.

Our canonical run for the electron uses 128 particles instead of the 256 for the ion. However the electron runs require that TEND be at least 2, and they are much longer than those for ions. A major success of the BETA transport code is its effectiveness in these electron calculations. The output shows, as explained in Chapter IV, that the expected value Γ of a suitable cosine defines the electron confinement time adequately over both half and full intervals of the run. The elapsed time is too short for the other expected values that are output to provide meaningful results, as is evidenced by the fact that no particles are lost. The electric field is input in Subroutine ELPOT by specifying formulas for Φ and its three first derivatives. Redundant coding of Φ should be avoided to maintain efficiency of the calculation.

Table 2 is the result of a study for the TJ-II Heliac at $\bar{\nu} = 64$. From the table we see that for zero electric field the electron confinement time was approximately 70 times greater than the ion confinement time. This factor was reduced by using just a radial term in the electric field, and then with the addition of a much smaller resonant term the confinement times became nearly equal. On the other hand, if we look at the entry with $P_{17,4} = -0.02$, which is not resonant, we note that the discrepancy has increased.

72

$P_{0,0}$	$P_{10,3}$	$P_{17,5}$	$P_{17,4}$	τ_i	τ_e	$C_{1,0}$	$C_{10,3}$	$C_{17,5}$
-3.0	0.00	0.00	0.00	150	350	-0.03	0.01	0.00
-1.5	-0.02	0.00	0.00	60	65	0.00	-0.03	0.00
-1.5	0.00	-0.02	0.00	65	40	0.02	0.06	-0.02
-1.5	0.00	0.00	-0.02	30	250	-0.04	0.03	0.02
-1.5	0.00	0.00	0.00	65	600	-0.04	0.00	0.00
-1.5	0.00	0.00	0.02	24	320	-0.04	-0.01	0.03
-1.5	0.00	0.02	0.00	120	90	0.01	-0.01	-0.02
-1.5	0.02	0.00	0.00	50	80	-0.07	-0.01	0.03
0.0	0.00	0.00	0.00	5	350	-0.05	0.02	-0.11

Table 2. Fourier coefficients $C_{m,n}$ of the charge separation

$$\langle F_i \rangle - \langle F_e \rangle = C_{1,0} \cos \tilde{\psi} + C_{10,3} \sin(10\tilde{\psi}-3\tilde{\phi}) + C_{17,5} \sin(17\tilde{\psi}-5\tilde{\phi})$$

versus Fourier coefficients $P_{m,n}$ of the electric potential

$$\Phi = P_{0,0}(1-s) + \Sigma\, P_{m,n} \sin(m\tilde{\psi}-n\tilde{\phi}),$$

which is measured in units of the temperature, for the TJ-II Heliac with $\bar{\nu}$ = 64 and β = 0.05, and with gyroradii ρ_i = 0.01 for ions and ρ_e = 0.0002 for electrons. The ion and electron confinement times τ_i and τ_e are given in milliseconds for a toroidal magnetic field B = 1 tesla, and the dimensionless collision frequency $\bar{\nu}$ = 1 for a typical reactor regime.

INPUT

NS	NPSI	NPHI	NMAG	NEK	NTE1	NTE2	TE1
4	4	2	2	2	1	1	0.9900

FREQ	FREQE	DELT	TEND	SEED	SIZEL	NPOL	NCOL
64.0000	64.0000	0.0025	2.0000	841.00	0.0080	2	1

RADL	E0	E1	E2	E3	ACC	MF	NF
-0.00020	-1.5000	0.0000	0.0000	-0.0200	5.0000	4	3

IC	NPRT	TLIM	NRUN	NSTU	NOFC		TITLE
20	-1	4000.0	300	0	6		TJ-II

FOURIER COEFFICIENTS OF DISTRIBUTION FUNCTION

M	N	K
0	1	0
1	-1	1
1	0	1
10	-7	0
3	-2	0
17	-12	0

DATA USED FROM EQUILIBRIUM RUN

EP	RBOU	QLZ	RUN
0.1140	1.0000	4.0000	1000

NI	NJ	NK	NIV	NVAC
13	36	36	0	-21

MF	NF	IROT	C1	C2
9	4	1	0.0000	0.0000

B0 = 1.012   AVERAGE PLASMA RADIUS = 1.119

	$C(M-N)$	$C(M+N)$	$S(M+N)$	$S(M-N)$
NUMBER OF FOURIER TERMS				
REPRESENTING MAGNETIC FIELD	7	8	0	0

FOURIER COEFFICIENTS OF DISTRIBUTION FUNCTION

(S**K/2)*COS(M*PSI-N*PHI)

TIME	0,1,0	1,-1,1	1,0,1	10,-7,0	3,-2,0	17,-12,0
12.254	0.164	0.195	0.113	0.108	-.111	-.028
12.504	0.135	0.168	0.125	0.080	-.096	0.028
12.754	0.107	0.173	0.133	0.067	-.121	0.048
13.004	0.107	0.172	0.135	0.065	-.133	0.046
13.254	0.108	0.169	0.138	0.040	-.131	0.038
13.504	0.104	0.173	0.143	0.021	-.137	0.024
13.754	0.102	0.179	0.148	0.000	-.151	0.014
14.004	0.111	0.181	0.148	-.010	-.136	0.006
14.254	0.109	0.177	0.141	-.020	-.119	0.007
14.504	0.111	0.180	0.144	-.016	-.110	0.006
14.754	0.110	0.178	0.144	-.006	-.094	0.009
15.004	0.106	0.175	0.138	-.003	-.093	0.010
15.254	0.113	0.178	0.140	0.005	-.102	0.016
15.504	0.106	0.178	0.145	0.023	-.107	0.015
15.754	0.102	0.178	0.144	0.024	-.104	0.015
16.004	0.097	0.175	0.144	0.014	-.098	0.007
16.254	0.093	0.175	0.144	0.011	-.094	0.007
16.504	0.086	0.175	0.147	0.012	-.084	0.011
16.754	0.083	0.168	0.147	0.015	-.075	0.013
17.004	0.083	0.166	0.150	0.012	-.070	0.008
17.254	0.082	0.162	0.150	0.005	-.071	-.004
17.504	0.078	0.160	0.153	0.008	-.072	-.010
17.754	0.080	0.161	0.151	0.010	-.063	-.013
18.004	0.082	0.157	0.149	0.017	-.059	-.018
18.254	0.083	0.160	0.147	0.019	-.055	-.024
18.504	0.084	0.159	0.144	0.018	-.050	-.031
18.754	0.086	0.158	0.143	0.016	-.048	-.035
19.004	0.085	0.155	0.137	0.016	-.040	-.036
19.254	0.084	0.153	0.136	0.016	-.035	-.035
19.504	0.085	0.150	0.133	0.017	-.037	-.035
19.754	0.082	0.147	0.135	0.018	-.040	-.033
20.004	0.082	0.142	0.133	0.019	-.043	-.029
20.254	0.085	0.139	0.129	0.017	-.047	-.023
20.504	0.086	0.136	0.128	0.018	-.043	-.019
20.754	0.087	0.132	0.130	0.021	-.037	-.016
21.004	0.087	0.130	0.131	0.024	-.033	-.013
21.254	0.086	0.130	0.132	0.029	-.029	-.010
21.504	0.085	0.131	0.132	0.037	-.029	-.008
21.754	0.084	0.130	0.131	0.042	-.030	-.009
22.004	0.084	0.132	0.131	0.046	-.032	-.012
22.254	0.084	0.130	0.131	0.046	-.031	-.012
22.504	0.084	0.132	0.131	0.047	-.031	-.016
22.754	0.082	0.133	0.130	0.045	-.029	-.019
23.004	0.084	0.131	0.129	0.043	-.028	-.020
23.254	0.081	0.133	0.127	0.039	-.030	-.018
23.504	0.080	0.133	0.129	0.039	-.030	-.016

FINAL RADL = 0.00021

OUTPUT

NUMBER LOST =   0   NUMBER REMAINING =   128

COLLISION TIME =   16.67   PERIODS TRAVERSED =   304.9

ENERCON =   7.741E-08   CPU TIME =   3438 S

MEAN FREE PATH / FIELD PERIOD =   24.0

CONFINEMENT TIME TAU AND LOSS RATE   1/TAU

ELECTRON CONFINEMENT TIME = 40   EQUIVALENT TO   40 MS AT 1 TESLA

1-S TEST FUNCTION

| | | | STANDARD |
TIME INTERVAL	TAU	LOSS RATE	DEVIATION
FULL INTERVAL 212.17	32.8	0.030	0.005
HALF INTERVAL 106.13	-8.5	-0.118	0.003

COSINE TEST FUNCTION

| | | | STANDARD |
TIME INTERVAL	TAU	LOSS RATE	DEVIATION
FULL INTERVAL 212.17	41.8	0.024	0.000
HALF INTERVAL 106.13	40.9	0.024	0.000

PARTICLE LOSS TEST FUNCTION

| | | | STANDARD |
TIME INTERVAL	TAU	LOSS RATE	DEVIATION
FULL INTERVAL 212.17	54083288.3	0.000	0.000
HALF INTERVAL 106.13	54083288.3	0.000	0.000

EXPONENTIAL DECAY OF EXPECTED VALUES

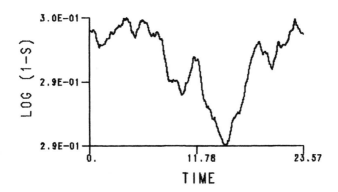

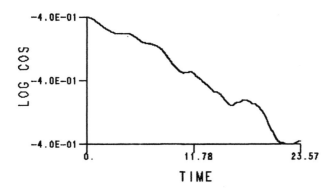

Fig. 26. Exponential decay for electrons showing increased difficulty of the computation and the advantage of using an expected value of the cosine functional Γ.

15. Confinement time for Heliotron E

The BETA transport code has been applied extensively to the Heliotron E experiment and comparisons have been made of the computed particle confinement time [5]. In this example the relevant parameters for the Monte Carlo method are the ion gyroradius RADL = 0.008 and the dimensionless collision frequency $\bar{\nu}$ = 16. We have put β = 0.002, EP = 0.1, and DEL2 = 0.3 for the equilibrium run. The toroidal field is B = 1 tesla and the computed ion confinement time turns out to be 70 ms. In the corresponding experiment the magnetic field was 0.95 tesla, the ion and electron temperatures were 175 eV, and the gross energy confinement time τ_E was 10 ms, so after suitable corrections have been made the comparison between these numbers would seem to be favorable [28]. In this computation the electric potential Φ has been set to zero, but a more elaborate table comparing ion and electron confinement times and determining the electric field from charge neutrality conditions has been published elsewhere [6].

In contrast to the previous electron run, the ion confinement time here is most reliably computed from the exponential decay of 1-s. Various results found for different expected values over two separate time intervals exhibit the uncertainty inherent in the Monte Carlo method. The particle loss rate listed in the output does not become relevant until about half of the particles have escaped. In Section IV.2 we demonstrate (cf. Fig. 32) that confinement times estimated from all three of the expected values we calculate ultimately approach more or less the same limit. In the present case the answers found over the second half of the run for 1-s and for the cosine function Γ agree quite well. The small standard deviation in the exponential fit to 1-s shows that the rate of decay is well established and has become independent of initial data.

INPUT

NS	NPSI	NPHI	NMAG	NEK	NTE1	NTE2	TE1
4	4	4	2	2	1	1	0.9900

FREQ	FREQE	DELT	TEND	SEED	SIZEL	NPOL	NCOL
16.0000	16.0000	0.0100	1.0000	121.00	0.0080	2	1

RADL	E0	E1	E2	E3	ACC	MF	NF
0.00800	0.0000	0.0000	0.0000	0.0000	5.0000	4	3

IC	NPRT	TLIM	NRUN	NSTU	NOFC	TITLE
20	-1	2400.0	300	0	1	HELIOTRON E

FOURIER COEFFICIENTS OF DISTRIBUTION FUNCTION

M	N	K
1	0	0

DATA USED FROM EQUILIBRIUM RUN

EP	RBOU	QLZ	RUN
0.1000	1.0000	18.0000	1

NI	NJ	NK	NIV	NVAC
13	24	24	0	-21

MF	NF	IROT	C1	C2
4	3	0	0.0000	0.0000

B0 = 1.191   AVERAGE PLASMA RADIUS = 1.023

	C(M-N)	C(M+N)	S(M+N)	S(M-N)
NUMBER OF FOURIER TERMS REPRESENTING MAGNETIC FIELD	6	2	0	0

OUTPUT

NUMBER LOST =   10   NUMBER REMAINING =   246

COLLISION TIME =   1.04   PERIODS TRAVERSED = 1441.6

ENERCON =   0.541E-05   CPU TIME = 1784 S

MEAN FREE PATH / FIELD PERIOD =   356.8

CONFINEMENT TIME TAU AND LOSS RATE   1/TAU

CONFINEMENT TIME =   73   EQUIVALENT TO   73 MS AT 1 TESLA

1-S TEST FUNCTION

		TAU	LOSS RATE	STANDARD DEVIATION
TIME INTERVAL				
FULL INTERVAL	4.21	42.2	0.024	0.025
HALF INTERVAL	2.11	75.7	0.013	0.006

COSINE TEST FUNCTION

		TAU	LOSS RATE	STANDARD DEVIATION
TIME INTERVAL				
FULL INTERVAL	4.21	61.4	0.016	0.006
HALF INTERVAL	2.11	73.2	0.014	0.003

PARTICLE LOSS TEST FUNCTION

		TAU	LOSS RATE	STANDARD DEVIATION
TIME INTERVAL				
FULL INTERVAL	4.21	110.8	0.009	0.158
HALF INTERVAL	2.11	183.0	0.005	0.084

EXPONENTIAL DECAY OF EXPECTED VALUES

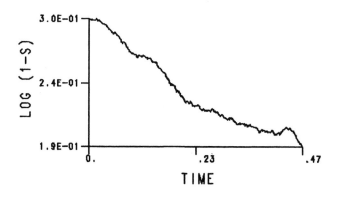

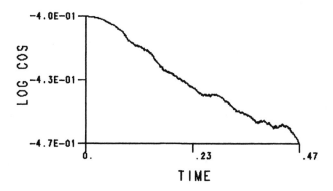

Fig. 27. Exponential decay of expected values of 1-s and of Γ for ion confinement in the Heliotron E at $\bar{\nu} = 16$.

III. REVISIONS OF THE EQUILIBRIUM CODE

1. Glossary for the equilibrium and stability code

The FORTRAN updates in Section 2 of this chapter eliminate several minor bugs in the equilibrium code, but the principal addition is Subroutine BOUNCE. This implements a simplified neoclassical transport theory defining the geometric confinement time output by the equilibrium code. The listing of the subroutine makes available all details of a method of bounce averaging that has turned out to be very successful in practice [8]. There are also changes designed to study resonance. Some improvements are included for the NGEOM = 4 option, and Subroutines ASIN and SURF are modified to incorporate a new NGEOM = 5 option. Updates occur in Subroutine PBOU which assist in defining the winding law for free boundary calculations.

The option NGEOM = 5 has been introduced in order to specify Heliac configurations in a more effective way than was possible using NGEOM = 3, which has now become obsolete. The plasma shape is defined by means of a trigonometric polynomial with a minimal number of terms. A theorem in conformal mapping shows that the Fourier coefficients Δ_{mn} defining the boundary of the plasma are determined uniquely in certain cases when NGEOM = 5 is used, and the parameter DELC emerges as a quantitative measure of the crescent or bean shape of the plasma cross section. The formula coded for NGEOM = 5 in Subroutine SURF is

$$r + iz = e^{iu} \sum \Delta_{mn} e^{-imu+inv} ,$$

where

$$u = UP1 + ALFU*SIN(UP1) + IROT*VP1, \quad v = VP1 .$$

Test functions for stability are modified when IROT = 1 because the coordinate system rotates with increasing v in that case.

CARDS 1,3,5,...   FORTRAN names of the parameters.

CARD 2

EP   The inverse of the aspect ratio. FORMAT F8.4.

RBOU   The ratio of the plasma radius to the wall
                         radius. For the fixed boundary case RBOU = 1.,
                         and for a free boundary we generally set RBOU
                         = 0.45. FORMAT F8.4.

QLZ   The number of field periods, or the cylinder
                         length if EP = 0. FORMAT F8.4.

NRUN   The number of field periods for which a
                         stability calculation is done. For equilibrium
                         runs NRUN = 1. For some stability studies we
                         have chosen NRUN so that NRUN times the
                         rotational transform at s = 1 is approximately
                         equal to 1. FORMAT I8.

NGEOM   This indicator selects the appropriate wall
                         geometry given in Subroutine SURF. NGEOM = 1
                         is the standard wall for a device like the
                         ATF-1, NGEOM = 2 selects a similar wall
                         description, NGEOM = 3 is obsolete, NGEOM = 4
                         selects a wall representation which permits
                         more Fourier terms for the Wendelstein VII-AS,
                         and NGEOM = 5 selects the wall for Heliac
                         devices. An additional Card 6A of input is
                         used for NGEOM = 4. FORMAT I8.

RUN   The number assigned to a run. FORMAT I8.

CARD 4

DEL0,DEL1,   The Fourier coefficients for the wall geometry.
DEL2,DEL3,   FORMAT 7F8.4.
DEL10,DEL20,
DEL30

CARD 6

DEL22,DEL33,   Additional coefficients for the wall.
DELA,DELB,   If NGEOM = 4 then the names of the coefficients
DELC   read in on Card 4, Card 6 and an additional
                         Card 6A are modified (cf. Section III.2).
                         FORMAT 5F8.4.

CARD 8

XPR,YPR,ZPR,PO   Parameters in $PO(1 - ZPR(SL2)^{YPR})^{XPR}$, which is
                         the pressure. FORMAT 4F8.4.

AMU0,AMU1,AMU2   Parameters initializing the rotational
                         transform AMU = AMU0 + AMU1*SL1 + AMU2*SL2. If
                         IROT = 1 then AMU = ι-1. The code may abort if
                         AMU is initialized inaccurately. FORMAT 3F8.4.

CARD 10

ALF

This parameter defines the mesh distribution in the radial direction. Suggested value for a fixed boundary case is 0.5 and for the free boundary case 0.0. FORMAT F8.4

ALFU

This zoning parameter helps redistribute the mesh so that it is equally spaced in the u direction. FORMAT F8.4.

CARD 12

NI

The number of s mesh points in the plasma region. FORMAT I8.

NJ

The number of u mesh points. FORMAT I8.

NK

The number of v mesh points. FORMAT I8.

ASYE

The axisymmetric convergence tolerance. Suggested value for a two-dimensional calculation 1.0E-04, for a three-dimensional calculation 1.0E+02. FORMAT E8.1.

ERR

Convergence tolerance for a three-dimensional calculation. Suggested value 1.0E-14. FORMAT E8.1.

CARD 14

SA1

The coefficient of the second time derivative of R in the acceleration scheme. Suggested value 4.0, but for harder cases 6.0. FORMAT F8.4.

SA2

The coefficient of the second time derivative of ψ in the acceleration scheme. Suggested value 4.0, but for difficult cases the scheme can be slowed down by taking SA2 = 8.0 or more. FORMAT F8.4.

SA3

The coefficient of the second time derivative of the magnetic axis. Suggested value 0.5. FORMAT F8.4.

DT

The artificial time step. Suggested value for the crude grid 0.02. DT scales like the mesh size divided by the square root of the Jacobian ratio. FORMAT F8.4.

CARD 16

SE1

The initial value of the descent coefficient for the plasma equation. Suggested value 300.0. FORMAT F8.4.

SEMU

This coefficient is used in the rotational transform iteration. Suggested value 0.5. FORMAT F8.4.

SEAX	This parameter is associated with the R equation on the magnetic axis. Suggested values in the range 2. $\leq$ SEAX $\leq$ 6. FORMAT F8.4.

CARD 18

SAFI	Constant in the acceleration scheme. Default value = 2.2. FORMAT F8.4.
NE	The number of points in an average for the descent coefficient. For most cases we use NE = 100. FORMAT I8.
NVAC	A constant which specifies the type of run. NVAC < 0 implies a fixed boundary run, NVAC > 0 implies a free boundary run, if ABS(NVAC) < 10 the rotational transform is held constant, for 10 < ABS(NVAC) < 30 the rotational transform is iterated, and for ABS(NVAC) > 30 the outer wall is perturbed to study islands. FORMAT I8.

CARD 20

NR,NZ	These indices are used to hold specified Fourier coefficients of the magnetic axis constant. FORMAT I8.
NT	If NT is positive an equilibrium run is made, but if NT is negative a stability run is made. Suggested value NT = 100 for equilibrium. For stability NT is negative and its numerical value gives the number of iterations for the equilibrium part of the run. FORMAT I8.
NAC	An indicator which is used to start the acceleration scheme. Suggested value NAC = 200. FORMAT I8.
DPSI	This is the magnitude of the perturbation for stability runs. Suggested values are DPSI = 0.2 for an m = 1 mode, DPSI = 0.05 for an m = 2 mode, and DPSI = 0.02 for an m = 3 mode. FORMAT F8.4.
GAM	The adiabatic gas constant γ . FORMAT F8.4.
IGAM	Defines the density in the norm used for stability. Suggested value IGAM = 1. FORMAT I8.

CARD 22

MIS,NIS	Print parameters. Suggested values MIS = 2, NIS = 1. FORMAT 2I8.
NAS	Selects the initial values of R for a three-dimensional run. If NAS > 0 the axisymmetric values are used, but if NAS < 0 a better approximation is computed. Suggested value -5. FORMAT I8.

| IROT | The coordinate system is rotated with v by IROT. This parameter appears in the formulas for NGEOM = 5. For the Heliac IROT = 1, otherwise it is usually zero. When IROT = 1 the code works with a modified rotational transform AMU = ι-1. FORMAT I8. |

MF,NF,IPF

These indices give the number of terms kept in the Fourier analysis for 1/B*B. Fourier coefficients are printed at NI = IPF. Suggested values are MF = NJ/4, NF = NK/4, and IPF = (NI+1)/2. FORMAT 3I8.

CARD 24

IC

Print parameter. Suggested value 50. FORMAT I8.

ITERF

The total number of iterations for equilibrium and stability. FORMAT I8.

TLIM

The CPU time limit in seconds. A value larger than the approximate length of the run should be input so that the run will be terminated by ITERF and not by exceeding TLIM. FORMAT F8.4.

CARD 26

PRINT1,
PRINT2,...,
PRINT8

Eight output parameters are selected on this card for printing each IC iterations. The choices appear in Subroutine PRNT. FORMAT 8A8.

CARD 28

USO

Phase in the winding law. USO = 0.5 for the Heliac, but usually USO = 0. FORMAT F8.4.

UIN

This shifts the poloidal harmonics in the Fourier analysis. Suggested value UIN = 0. FORMAT F8.4

USM

This parameter prescribes the type of boundary condition for the potential on the outer wall in the free boundary case. A Dirichlet condition is prescribed over the entire boundary if USM < 0. For USM > 0 a Dirichlet condition is applied in the interval USM ≤ U ≤ 1-USM and a Neumann condition is applied on the remainder of the boundary. Suggested value USM = -1. FORMAT F8.4.

IVAX

If IVAX < 0 the vacuum axis is not iterated, but if IVAX > 0 it is iterated. FORMAT I8.

BULGE

The amplitude of a sine modulation of the scalar potential in the toroidal direction in the winding law. FORMAT F8.4.

TILT

The amplitude of a sine modulation of the scalar potential in the poloidal direction in the winding law. Suggested values in the range -0.2 ≤ TILT ≤ 0.2. FORMAT F8.4.

COIL Parameter used to modulate the poloidal coil location. FORMAT F8.4.

CARD 30

NIV The number of s mesh points in the vacuum region. We use NIV = NI for NVAC > 0 and NIV = 1 for NVAC < 0. FORMAT I8.

NV The number of vacuum iterations for each free boundary iteration. Suggested value NV = 3. FORMAT I8.

NP The number of plasma iterations for each free boundary iteration. Suggested value NP = 1. FORMAT I8.

OM The relaxation factor for Laplace's equation in the vacuum region. OM is scaled with mesh size H like 2./(1+H*const.), where OM = 1.6 for the crude 7×12×12 grid. FORMAT F8.4.

SAFV Default value SAFV = 2.0. FORMAT F8.4.

SE4 The descent coefficient for the free boundary equation. Suggested value 1.0. FORMAT F8.4.

C1 The toroidal current. C1 = 0 for stellarators. FORMAT F8.4.

C2 The poloidal current. Suggested value for EP > 0 is C2 = 2π/(EP*QLZ) and for EP = 0 is C2 = QLZ. This value is adjusted so that BTOR is approximately 1 for all s. FORMAT F8.4.

CARD 32

KW1,KW2,AK3, These parameters help to define the winding
TORS law. For the Heliac with only one coil KW1 = 1 and KW2 = 0. For the Heliotron E, which is an ℓ = 2 stellarator, KW1 = 2 and KW2 = 1. Generally AK3 = 1 and TORS = 0. FORMAT 4F8.4.

AMPH This is an amplitude in the winding law defined in Subroutine PBOU. Suggested value in the range -0.7 ≤ AMPH ≤ -0.3. FORMAT F8.4.

EVERT An indicator for the vertical field iteration. If EVERT < 0 the vertical field is fixed, but if EVERT > 0 the vertical field is iterated. Suggested value -1. FORMAT F8.4.

WRAD A smoothing parameter for the winding law equal to 1/XR. It helps to shape the plasma. Suggested value -1.5. FORMAT F8.4.

VERT The vertical field strength. Suggested value VERT = 0. FORMAT F8.4.

CARD 34

| NRA1,NRA2, NZA1,NZA2 | These parameters select Fourier coefficients of the magnetic axis to be plotted on completion of the calculation. The choices are given in Subroutine FPRNT. FORMAT 4I8. |

MK1,MK2,
MK3,MK4

The indices of the Fourier coefficients of R which are plotted. FORMAT 4I8.

CARD 36

EL1,EL2

The coefficients in the stability test function for DELRO. For m = 1, EL1 = 1 and EL2 = 0. For other modes EL1 = 0 and EL2 = 0. FORMAT 2F8.4.

EM1,EM2

The coefficients in the stability test function DELZO. For m = 1, EM1 = 1 and EM2 = 0. For all other modes EM1 = 0 and EM2 = 0. FORMAT 2F8.4.

M,N

These are used just as a label to identify the mode under consideration. FORMAT 2I8.

CARD 38

EAM1,EAM2,
EAM3

The coefficients of DELRAD in the test function for stability. They are EAMC1, EAMC2, and EAMC3 inside the code. For the test function coded, when m = 1 we put EAM1 = 2.0, EAM2 = 0.0, EAM3 = 0.0 and when m = 2 we put EAM1 = 0.0, EAM2 = 2.0, EAM3 = 0.0, but when m = 3 we put EAM1 = 0.0, EAM2 = 0.0, EAM3 = 2.0. FORMAT 3F8.4.

EAM4,EAM5,
EAM6

The coefficients of DELPSI in the test function for stability. They are EAMC4, EAMC5, and EAMC6 inside the code. For the test function coded, when m=1 we put EAM4 = -1.0, EAM5 = 0.0, EAM6 = 0.0, and when m = 2 we put EAM4 = 0.0, EAM5 = -1.0, EAM6 = 0.0, but when m = 3 we put EAM4 = 0.0, EAM5 = 0.0, EAM6 = -1.0. FORMAT 3F8.4.

2. FORTRAN update

The following are updates of the equilibrium and stability code listed in a previous publication [4], and the page numbers below refer to that book.

Page 85, replace line 30 in CLICHE NAMEB by
    PARAMETER(ID=NID,JD=NJD+2,KD=NKD*NRUND+2,IV=NIVD,JD2=2*NJD+2,
    1KD2=2*NKD*NRUND+2)

Page 87, replace line 18 in CLICHE NAME10 by
    4 SPPVOL(ID), AMS(ID), MIS1, MIS, NIS, NAS,MF,NF,IPF,AMAGM,IRP

Page 87, replace line 35 in CLICHE NAME13 by
    2 PO2, SEAX, USM, IVAX, BULGE, TILT, COIL

Page 87, replace line 40 in CLICHE NAME14 by
    2,DELA,DELB,DELC,YPR,ZPR,ALFU2,ALFU3

Page 88, replace line 11 in CLICHE NAME20 by
    COMMON /TEST/ MMODE,NMODE,EAMC1,EAMC2,EAMC3,EAMC4,EAMC5,EAMC6

Page 88, replace lines 19,20,and 21 in CLICHE NAME21 by
    1,TRAP1(ID,11),PHU1(ID,KD),PHV1(ID,KD),PHD(ID,KD),PHB2(ID,KD)
    1,PPRIM(ID),AWN(ID),BS2(ID),BS4(ID),DAV1(10),DAV2(10),DIFC1(ID,10,
    1,BSAV(ID),TRAP(ID,11),SNLP(ID,11),BMAGM(ID,11),NMO,BRIP(ID)
    1,XPA(11),DXPA(11),ERRL(11),DENS(ID),DIFC(ID,10),FREC(20),ANUP
    1,QLZ,IPTR,BOUC(ID),TNO(ID),DCIR(ID,10),DCIR1(ID,10),ZTO(ID)

Page 88, replace line 27 in CLICHE NAME22 by
    1,FILJ(JD),FILK(KD),COSPSI(11),SINPSI(11),COSPHI(7),SINPHI(7)
    1,GS2(11,7,4)

Page 89, in the main routine replace line 16 by
    IF (NGEOM.EQ.4) go to 10

Page 89, for NGEOM = 4 insert after line 26
    READ (25,1720)
    READ (25,1680) DELO,ALFU2,ALFU3

Page 89, to implement the winding law replace line 52 by
    READ (25,1460) USO,UIN,USM,IVAX,BULGE,TILT,COIL

Page 90, insert after line 21
    PRINT 1771, DELO,ALFU2,ALFU3

Page 90,to restrict MF and NF insert after line 28
    IF(MF.GT.NJ/4)MF=NJ/4
    IF(NF.GT.NK/4)NF=NK/4

Page 90, replace line 35 by
    PRINT 1500,USO,UIN,USM,IVAX,BULGE,TILT,COIL

Page 90, replace line 39 by
    PRINT 1891, EL1,EL2,EM1,EM2,MMODE,NMODE

Page 90, for additional output insert after line 48

89

```
        IPTR=-1

Page 92, insert after line 32
        IRP=-1

Page 94, to study resonance insert after line 53
        IF (ND.GT.30) GO TO 360

Page 95, insert after line 13
        IF (ITER.GT.NT1.AND.ND.GT.30) GO TO 880

Page 96, insert after line 1
        IF (ND.LE.30) GO TO 580
        IRP=1
        DO 579 K=2,N5
        DO 579 J=1,N2
        R(J,K)=R(J,K)+EL1*EF1(J,K)
        RU(J,K)=RU(J,K)+EL1*EF2(J,K)
        RV(J,K)=RV(J,K)+EL1*EF3(J,K)
        Z(J,K)=Z(J,K)+EL2*EG1(J,K)
        ZU(J,K)=ZU(J,K)+EL2*EG2(J,K)
        ZV(J,K)=ZV(J,K)+EL2*EG3(J,K)
    579 CONTINUE
        GO TO 661

Page 97, delete line 6

Page 97, insert after line 8
        X1=DPSI/PNORM
    661 CONTINUE
        ENERZ=ETOT

Page 97, replace line 14 by
        IF(ND.GT.30) X1=0.0

Page 97, insert after line 29
        IF(ND.GT.30) GO TO 880

Page 103, to save data for transport replace line 53 by
        WRITE (7) NVAC,NI,NJ,NK,NUMB,IROT

Page 104, replace line 1 by
        WRITE (7) HS,HU,HV,EP,QLZ,RBOU,ZLE,PI

Page 104, insert after line 3
        WRITE (7) ((RV(J,K),J=1,N2),K=1,N5),((ZV(J,K),J=1,N2),K=1,N5)

Page 104, insert after line 7
        WRITE (7) (SL2(I),I=I,NI),(PC(I),I=1,NI),(TC(I),I=1,NI)

Page 104, replace line 14 through 23 by
        CALL FPRINT(ITER,1)
        WRITE (7) (PR(I),I=2,N3),(PPRIM(I),I=2,N3)
        WRITE (7) (BRIP(I),I=1,NI),(QQ(I),I=1,NI)

Page 104, replace line 27 by
   1460 FORMAT (3F8.4,I8,3F8.4)

Page 104, replace line 32 by
   1500 FORMAT(13X,3HUSO,5X,3HUIN,5X,3HUSM,4X,4HIVAX,3X,5HBULGE,4X,4HTILT
      1,4X,4HCOIL/8X,3F8.4,3X,I5,3F8.4//)
```

Page 105, insert after line 12
1771 FORMAT(12X,4HDELO,3X,5HALFU2,3X,5HALFU3/9X,3(F7.4,1X)//)

Page 117, for NGEOM = 5 insert after line 30
IROT=IROT*NRUN

Page 120, to initialize axis correctly insert after line 39
IF(X1.GT.0.001. AND.NVAC.LT.0) GO TO 32
DO 31 K=2,N4
RPAX(K)=ROAX(K)
RPBX(K)=ROBX(K)
RPCX(K)=ROCX(K)
31 CONTINUE
RETURN
32 CONTINUE

Page 121, insert after line 17
RPAX(K)=ROAX(K)
RPBX(K)=ROBX(K)
RPCX(K)=ROCX(K)

Page 136, replace line 20 by
2 01), AZZ(101), ABZ(101), AW(101), AITP(101), AMER(101)
Page 136, replace line 45 by
TLAM(I)=1.0/X1

Page 137, to obtain current insert after line 8
ZTO(I)=0.0

Page 137, to fix a bug in Subroutine CDEN replace line 19 by
Y5=(PC(I+1)-PC(I-1))/Y3
Y6=(TC(I+1)-TC(I-1))/Y3
FACP(I)=TLAM(I)*(TC(I)*Y5+PC(I)*Y6)

Page 139, insert after line 44
ZTO(I)=ZTO(I)+HU*HV*UV1(I,K)

Page 140, insert after line 25
BSAV(I)=0.5*(BMAX(I)+BMIN(I))

Page 140, insert after line 26
WRITE (2) (ZTO(I),I=2,N3),(BMAX(I),I=2,N3),(BMIN(I),I=2,N3)

Page 142, replace lines 30 and 31 by
USE NAME14
DIMENSION FP(101),ABBF(101),ABJF(101),AZZF(101)
DIMENSION SCL(4),ALP(101),FACP(101),ACO(10,10),BCO(10),CCO(10),
1AWCO(10,10),WKS1(10),WKS2(10),FCO(10),NFC(20)

Page 142, in Subroutine FPHI for transport insert after line 35
NFC(1)=0
DO 1 N=2,NFT
1 NFC(N)=N-1
IF(IRP.LT.0) GO TO 3
NFT1=NFT
DO 2 N=2,NFT
IF((N-1)*NRUN.LE.NFC(NFT)) GO TO 2
NFT1=NFT1+1
NFC(NFT1)=(N-1)*NRUN
2 CONTINUE
NFT=NFT1

```
      NF=NFT
    3 CONTINUE
      VT=0.5
      DO 4 I=1,10
      X1=1.0*(-1.5+(I-1.5)/3.0)
    4 FREC(I)=10.0**X1
      X1=BNORM(1,NI,SL2,QQ,SL1(1),SL1(NI))
      ANUP=VT*RBOU*X1*PI/ZLE

Page 143, insert after line 2
      TOT=0.0

Page 143, replace line 17 by
      BSAV(I)=BSAV(I)+HU*HV*B2(J,K)*B2(J,K)
      TOT=TOT+HU*HV*B2(J,K)

Page 143, replace line 19 by
      BSAV(I)=SQRT(BSAV(I)/TOT)
      N33=N3-1
      II=(NI+1)/2
      IF(I.EQ.II.OR.I.EQ.N33) GO TO 31
      GO TO 35
   31 IF(I.EQ.II) GO TO 33
      DO 32 J=2,N1
      DO 32 K=2,N4
   32 XO(NI,J,K)=B2(J,K)
      GO TO 35
   33 DO 34 J=2,N1
      DO 34 K=2,N4
   34 XO(1,J,K)=B2(J,K)
   35 CONTINUE

Page 144, replace lines 14 through 47 by
      RT=(1.0-BRIP(I))/(1.0+BRIP(I))
      X1=SQRT(1.0-RT)
      DXPA(1)=(1.0-X1)/4.0
      DXPA(2)=DXPA(1)
      DXPA(3)=DXPA(1)
      DXPA(4)=DXPA(1)
      XPA(1)=1.0-0.5*DXPA(1)
      XPA(2)=XPA(1)-DXPA(1)
      XPA(3)=XPA(2)-DXPA(2)
      XPA(4)=XPA(3)-DXPA(3)
      DXPA(5)=X1
      XPA(5)=SQRT(BRIP(I))
      DXPA(6)=X1
      XPA(6)=SQRT(BRIP(I))
      DENS(I)=0.0
      DO 296 NM=1,5
      TRAP(I,NM)=0.0
      TRAP1(I,NM)=0.0
      SNLP(I,NM)=0.0
      BMAGM(I,NM)=1.0-XPA(NM)*XPA(NM)
      TOT2=0.0
      TOT=0.0
      TOT1=0.0
      FACMU=BSAV(I)*(1.0-BRIP(I))
      DO 151 J=2,N1
      DO 151 K=2,N4
      X5=SQRT(B2(J,K))
      X6=BMAGM(I,NM)*X5/FACMU
```

```
151    V1(J,K)=RBOU*SQRT(AMAX1(0.0,1.0-X6))/X5
       DO 160 M=1,MFT
       DO 160 N=1,NFT
       DO 160 L=1,4
       SCL(L)=0.0
       GS2(M,N,L)=0.0
       BB(M,N,L)=0.0
       OL(M,N,L)=0.0
160    BL(M,N,L)=0.0
C      COMPUTE FOURIER COEFFICIENTS OF 1/(B*B) AND PARALLEL CURRENT
       DO 180 J=2,N1
       DO 180 K=2,N4
       DO 161 M=1,MFT
       COSPSI(M)=COS((M-1)*PSI(J,K))
161    SINPSI(M)=SIN((M-1)*PSI(J,K))
       DO 162 N=1,NFT
       COSPHI(N)=COS(NFC(N)*PHI(J,K))
162    SINPHI(N)=SIN(NFC(N)*PHI(J,K))
       DO 180 M=1,MFT
       DO 180 N=1,NFT
       CL(1)=COSPSI(M)*COSPHI(N)
       CL(2)=COSPSI(M)*SINPHI(N)
       CL(3)=SINPSI(M)*COSPHI(N)
       CL(4)=SINPSI(M)*SINPHI(N)
       DO 170 L=1,4
       FAC2=FAC1*D(J,K)*CL(L)
       SCL(L)=SCL(L)+FAC2*B2(J,K)
       BB(M,N,L)=B(M,N,L)+FAC2
       GS2(M,N,L)=GS2(M,N,L)+FAC2*B2(J,K)/V3(J,K)
170    OL(M,N,L)=OL(M,N,L)+FAC2*B2(J,K)*V1(J,K)
180    CONTINUE

Page 144, insert after line 52
       GS2(M,1,L)=GS2(M,1,L)/2.0

Page 145, insert after line 3
       GS2(1,N,L)=GS2(1,N,L)/2.0

Page 145, replace lines 21 through 25 by
       X1=-((M-1)*PC(I)+NFC(N)*TC(I))/QT(I)
       X3=-((M-1)*PC(I)-NFC(N)*TC(I))/QT(I)
       X4=NFC(N)+(M-1.0)*Q(I)/QT(I)
       IF(ABS(X4).LT.AMUL)X4=SIGN(AMUL,X4)
       X2=NFC(N)-(M-1.)*Q(I)/QT(I)

Page 146, for simplified transport replace lines 14 through 47 by
       DO 281 J=2,N1
       DO 281 K=2,N4
       U1(J,K)=0.0
       X0(I,J,K)=0.0
       XL(1,J,K)=0.0
       DO 261 M=1,MFT
       COSPSI(M)=COS((M-1)*PSI(J,K))
261    SINPSI(M)=SIN((M-1)*PSI(J,K))
       DO 262 N=1,NFT
       COSPHI(N)=COS(NFC(N)*PHI(J,K))
262    SINPHI(N)=SIN(NFC(N)*PHI(J,K))
       DO 280 M=1,MFT
       DO 280 N=1,NFT
       CL(1)=COSPSI(M)*COSPHI(N)
       CL(2)=COSPSI(M)*SINPHI(N)
```

```
       CL(3)=SINPSI(M)*COSPHI(N)
       CL(4)=SINPSI(M)*SINPHI(N)
       DO 270 L=1,4
       XL(1,J,K)=XL(1,J,K)+CL(L)*OL(M,N,L)
       U1(J,K)=U1(J,K)+CL(L)*RL(M,N,L)
  270  XO(I,J,K))=XO(I,J,K)+CL(L)*BL(M,N,L)
  280  CONTINUE
  281  CONTINUE
  284  CONTINUE
       DO 290 J=2,N1
       DO 290 K=2,N4
       X1=HU*HV*GL(J,K)/V3(J,K)
       X2=XO(I,J,K)*FP(I)+FACP(I)
  C    COMPUTE INTEGRALS FOR THE MERCIER CRITERION
       ABBF(I)=ABBF(I)+X1
       ABJF(I)=ABJF(I)+X1*X2
       AZZF(I)=AZZF(I)+X1*X2*X2
       X5=SQRT(B2(J,K))
       X6=BMAGM(I,NM)*X5/FACMU
       TOT=TOT+HU*HV*GL(J,K)
       TOT1=TOT1+HU*HV*D(J,K)
       IF(1.0-X6.GT.0.0) GO TO 285
       TRAP(I,NM)=TRAP(I,NM)+HU*HV*D(J,K)
       TOT2=TOT2+HU*HV*GL(J,K)
       GO TO 290
  285  CONTINUE
       ALP(I)=ALP(I)+X1*U1(J,K)*U1(J,K)
  290  CONTINUE
       TRAP(I,NM)=(TOT1-TRAP(I,NM))/TOT1
       TRAP1(I,NM)=(TOT-TOT2)/TOT
       SNLP(I,NM)=(ALP(I)+0.0001)*FAC/(4.0*RBOU*RBOU)
       IF(I.NE.N33) GO TO 296
       IF(NM.LE.5) GO TO 296
       NS=1
       IF(NJ.GT.16)NS=1+NJ/16
       PRINT 291,I,BMAGM(I,NM)
  291  FORMAT(//,3X,"LAMDA PAR AT I=",I2,3X,"MAG MOMENT=",F5.3,//)
       DO 292 K=2,N4
  292  PRINT 293,(U1(J,K),J=2,N1,NS)
  293  FORMAT(3X,16F7.2)
       PRINT 294
  294  FORMAT(//,3X,"RHO PAR",//)
       DO 295 K=2,N4
  295  PRINT 293,(V1(J,K),J=2,N1,NS)
  296  CONTINUE
       NRUN1=1
       IF(IRP.GT.0)NRUN1=NRUN
       IF(BRIP(I).LT.0.001) GO TO 297
       AMUP=Q(I)/QT(I)+IROT*NRUN1
       CALL BOUNCE(I,FACMU,BMAGM(I,5),ANUB,DTOT,SNLP(I,5),FTOT,FTOTM,
      1AMUP,NFC)
       GO TO 298
  297  SNLP(I,5)=0.0
       ANUB=1.0
       DXPA(5)=0.0
  298  CONTINUE
       BOUC(I)=ANUB
       DCIR(I,1)=0.0
       DO 299 NM=1,4
       DCIR(I,1)=DCIR(I,1)+DXPA(NM)*SNLP(I,NM)
  299  DENS(I)=DENS(I)+DXPA(NM)*TRAP1(I,NM)
```

```
       DENP=DENS(I)
       DENS(I)=DENS(I)+DXPA(5)*TRAP1(I,5)
       DCIR1(I,1)=DCIR(I,1)*0.04/DENP
       DCIR(I,1)=DCIR(I,1)/DENS(I)
       DCIR(I,2)=DXPA(5)*SNLP(I,5)/DENS(I)
       TNO(I)=DXPA(5)
       DO 300 J=1,10
       X1=ANUP*FREC(J)
       X2=ANUB/X1
       DIFC1(I,J)=X1*(DCIR(I,1)+X2*X2*DCIR(I,2))
   300 CONTINUE
       RETURN
       END
```

Page 147, before top line insert Subroutine BOUNCE as follows:

```
       SUBROUTINE BOUNCE(II,FACMU,BMU,ANUT,DTOT,DTOTM,FTOT,FTOTM,AMUP,
      1NFC)
C      COMPUTATION OF BOUNCE FREQUENCY FOR TRAPPED PARTICLES
       USE NAME21
       USE NAME22
       USE NAME12
       USE NAME10
       USE NAME14
       USE NAME1
       DIMENSION NU(21),ANUB(21,21),COPS(20),SIPS(20),COPH(10),SIPH(10)
       DIMENSION NFC(20)
       FAC=-2.0*PI/(PC(II)*QT(II)+TC(II)*Q(II))
       FAC1=FAC*PC(II)
       FAC2=8.0/(PI*PI)
       X1=1.0/(ABS(AMUP)+0.0001)
       IF(IRP.GT.0) X1=X1*NRUN
       NQ=INT(X1)
       NQ=MAX0(NQ,1)
       IF(NQ.GT.50)NQ=50
       IF(NQ.LT.3)NQ=4*NQ
       IF(NQ.LT.6)NQ=2*NQ
       PHIL=PC(II)*NQ
       IF(IRP.GT.0) PHIL=PHIL/NRUN
       MFT=MF
       NFT=NF
       NTOT=0
       ANUT=0.0
       DTOT=0.0
       FTOT=0.0
       FTOTM=0.0
       NPSI=8
       DF=PC(II)/16.0
       IF(IRP.GT.0)DF=DF/NRUN
       DO 10 I=1,NPSI
       PSITO=2.0*PI*(I-1)/NPSI
       PSIO=PSITO/FAC1
       PHIO=-DF
       NU(I)=0
       ISO=0
       IND=0
     1 SUM=0.0
       SUMF=0.0
       SDF=0.0
       SLP1=0.0
       SLP2=0.0
       FTI=0.0
```

```
2   IF(PHIO.GT.PHIL) GO TO 10
    PHIO=PHIO+DF
    FTOTM=FTOTM+DF
    PSIT=FAC*(PC(II)*PSIO-Q(II)*PHIO)
    PHIT=FAC*(-QT(II)*PHIO-TC(II)*PSIO)
    DO 3 M=1,MFT
    COPS(M)=COS((M-1)*PSIT)
3   SIPS(M)=SIN((M-1)*PSIT)
    DO 4 N=1,NFT
    COPH(N)=COS(NFC(N)*PHIT)
4   SIPH(N)=SIN(NFC(N)*PHIT)
    BM=0.0
    S2=0.0
    ALMP=0.0
    DO 6 M=1,MFT
    DO 6 N=1,NFT
    CL(1)=COPS(M)*COPH(N)
    CL(2)=COPS(M)*SIPH(N)
    CL(3)=SIPS(M)*COPH(N)
    CL(4)=SIPS(M)*SIPH(N)
    DO 5 L=1,4
    S2=S2+CL(L)*GS2(M,N,L)
    ALMP=ALMP+CL(L)*RL(M,N,L)
5   BM=BM+CL(L)*BB(M,N,L)
6   CONTINUE
    IF(BM.GT.0.0) GO TO 7
    PRINT 32,BM,II,I,PSIT,PHIT
    STOP 33
7   CONTINUE
    BM=SQRT(1.0/BM)
    X6=BMU*BM/FACMU
    IF(1.0-X6.GT.0.0) GO TO 8
    IF(ISO.LE.0) GO TO 2
    ISO=-1
    IND=-1
    IF(SUMF.LT.0.0001) GO TO 2
    NU(I)=NU(I)+1
    NTOT=NTOT+1
    ANUB(I,NU(I))=FAC2*SUM/(SUMF*SUMF)
    ANUT=ANUT+ANUB(I,NU(I))
    X1=ANUT/NTOT
    X2=PSIT/(2.0*PI)
    X3=PHIT/(2.0*PI)
    DT1=SLP2-(SLP1*SLP1)/SDF
    FTOT=FTOT+FT1
    DTOT=DTOT+DT1*(ANUB(I,NU(I))**2.0)
    X4=DTOT/(FTOT*X1*X1)
    X5=DT1/FT1
    FPS=SLP1/SDF
    IF(NU(I).GT.10) GO TO 10
    GO TO 1
8   IF(ISO.LT.0) IND=1
    ISO=1
    IF(IND)9,2,9
9   SUM=SUM+DF*SQRT(1.0-X6)/BM
    SUMF=SUMF+DF/BM
    SDF=SDF+DF*S2
    SLP1=SLP1+S2*ALMP*DF
    SLP2=SLP2+S2*ALMP*ALMP*DF
    FT1=FT1+DF
    GO TO 2
```

```
 10  CONTINUE
     ANUT=ANUT/NTOT
     DTOTM=DTOT/(FTOTM*ANUT*ANUT)
     DTOT=DTOT/(FTOT*ANUT*ANUT)
 32  FORMAT(///,3X,"NEGATIVE BM=",F6.3,3X,2I5,2F6.2)
     RETURN
     END
```

Page 161, replace line 31 by
```
     8 SIMK4(50), SAMK4(50), NITER(50),CONF(50)
```

Page 161, replace line 43 by
```
     2 01), AZZ(101), ABZ(101), AW(101), AITP(101), AMER(101)
```

Page 163, insert after line 12
```
     IF(IABS(NVAC).GT.30) GO TO 81
```

Page 163, insert after line 13
```
 81  CONTINUE
```

Page 163, insert after line 17
```
     NRUN1=1
     IF(IRP.GT.0)NRUN1=NRUN
```

Page 164, replace line 43 by
```
     IF(IABS(NVAC.GT.30) GO TO 221
     IF(NT.LT.0. AND.NEQ.GT.0) GO TO 350
 221 CONTINUE
```

Page 165, delete line 15

Page 165, replace lines 17 through 19 by
```
     ANB1=RBOU*BNORM(3,N33,SL2,PLAM1,SL1(3),SL1(N33))/X1
     ANLB1=RBOU*BNORM(3,N33,SL2,PLAM2,SL1(3),SL1(N33))/X1
```

Page 165, delete lines 52 and 53

Page 166, in Subroutine FPRINT replace lines 1 through 4 by
```
 257 CONTINUE
     GO TO 270
 258 CONTINUE
     DO 261 J=1,10
     DO 260 I=2,N3
 260 ALP(I)=1.0/(SQRT(DIFC1(I,J))+0.000001)
     CONF(J)=BNORM(3,N33,SL2,ALP,SL1(3),SL1(N33))
 261 CONF(J)=1.0*CONF(J)*CONF(J)
     DO 262 I=2,N3
 262 ALP(I)=1.0/SQRT(DCIR1(I,1)+0.000001)
     CONF(11)=BNORM(3,N33,SL2,ALP,SL1(3),SL1(N33))
     CONF(11)=1.0*CONF(11)*CONF(11)
     DO 263 J=1,10
     X1=ANUP*FREC(J)
     COMU(J)=ALOG10(1.0/CONF(J))
 263 SD(J)=ALOG10(X1)
     DO 264 I=1,51
 264 SP(I)=SD(1)+(I-1)*(SD(10)-SD(1))/50.0
     CALL SPLIF(1,10,SD,CONF,FP,FPP,FPPP,3,0.0,3,0.0,0,0.0,IND)
     CALL INTPL(1,51,SP,SLMK3,1,10,SD,CONF,FP,FPP,FPPP,0)
     TAUM=0.0
     ANUM=0.0
     DO 265 I=1,51
```

```
        IF(SLMK3(I).LT.TAUM) GO TO 265
        TAUM=SLMK3(I)
        ANUM+10.0**SP(I)
265     CONTINUE
        PRINT 1265
        BSQ=BNORM(3,N33,SL2,BSAV,SL1(3),SL1(N33))
        BSQ=BSQ*BSQ
        TAUP=TAUM/BSQ
        CONFG=CONF(11)/BSQ
        PRINT 1273,CONFG,TAUP
        GO TO 341
270     CONTINUE
```

Page 166, insert after line 45
```
        GO TO 258
341     CONTINUE
```

Page 168, replace line 1 by
```
        PRINT 1090
```

Page 168, replace line 38 by
```
570     FORMAT(//,22X,"J*B/B*B ",21X,"JACOBIAN",/)
```

PAGE 168, replace lines 41 and 42 by
```
590     FORMAT(7X,F7.3,37X,2F10.3)
600     FORMAT(7X,F7.3,3X,3F10.3,4X,2F10.3)
```

Page 168, replace line 48 by
```
640     FORMAT(7X,F7.3,5X,3(F10.4,3X),5X,6(F10.4,3X))
```

Page 169, replace line 28 by
```
1S="F5.2//)
```

Page 170, insert after line 16
```
1265    FORMAT(////,42X,"GEOMETRIC CONFINEMENT TIME TAU",/)
1273    FORMAT(//,35X,"TAU CLASSICAL=",F7.2,5X,
       1"TAU PLATEAU=",F7.2,/)
```

Page 172, insert after line 4
```
        USE NAMEB
```

Page 172, replace line 16 by
```
2 01), AZZ(101), ABZ(101), AW(101), AITP(101),AMER(101)
```

Page 183, in Subroutine PBOU insert after line 15
```
        Y3=TILT*SIN(UP1)
```

Page 183, insert after line 18
```
        XR1=XR/(1.-COIL*COS(VP1))
```

Page 183, for winding law insert after line 20
```
        Y4=BULGE*SIN(VP1)
```

Page 183, replace lines 22 through 24 by
```
        X1=XR1*SIN(YY)/(1.0-XR1*COS(YY))
        SUM=ATAN(X1)/XR1
70      PT(NIV,J,K)=Y2+C2*V+SUM*AMPH+Y3+Y4
```

Page 184, for NGEOM = 5 in Subroutine ASIN replace line 33 by
```
        FQ1=FQ
        IF(NGEOM.NE.5) GO TO 41
```

```
          X1=2.0*PI*(DEL1+DELC-DEL33)/ZLE
          FQ1=FQ*(DELB*DELB+2.0*DELC*DELC-DEL22*DEL22)
          FQ=FQ1/SQRT(1.0+X1*X1)
       41 AA=AMAX1(ABS(AMU0),ABS(AMU1),ABS(AMU2))

Page 185, replace line 19 by
          AM(I)=(PRES**GUM)*FQ1

Page 185, replace line 32 by
      110 SNL2(I)=SNL2(I-1)+X1*(SL2(I)-SL2(I-1))/FQ

Page 186, insert after line 7
          USE NAME7

Page 186, for NGEOM = 5 in Subroutine SURF insert after line 15
          DIMENSION DELMM(10),DELMO(5),DELM(5)
          N=1
          DELMM(1)=DEL10
          DELMM(2)=-DELC
          DELMM(3)=-DELB
          DELMM(4)=-DEL1
          DELMM(5)=DEL22
          DELMM(6)=DEL33
          DELMM(7)=DELA
          DELM(1)=DEL2
          DELM(2)=DEL3
          DELMO(1)=DEL20
          DELMO(2)=DEL30

Page 186, replace line 42 by
          IF(NGEOM.EQ.4) GO TO 40
          IF(NGEOM.EQ.5) GO TO 51

Page 186, insert after line 52
          GO TO 60
       51 CONTINUE
          DELIN=DEL1+DELC-DEL33
          RA(K)=DELIN*X3
          ZA(K)=DELIN*X2

Page 187, replace line 25 by
          GO TO (110,120,80,90,101), NGEOM

Page 187, for NGEOM = 4 insert after line 47
          UBAR=UBAR+ALFU2*SIN(2.0*UP1)+ALFU3*SIN(2.0*UP1-VP1)
          UBARP=UBARP+PI2*(2.0*ALFU2*COS(2.0*UP1)+2.0*ALFU3*COS(2.0*UP1-
         1VP1))
          UBARPV=-ALFU3*PI2*COS(2.0*UP1-VP1)

Page 188, replace lines 3 and 4 by
          XX1=COS(L*UBAR-(M-1)*VP1)*DEL(L,M)
          XX2=SIN(L*UBAR-(M-1)*VP1)*DEL(L,M)

Page 188, replace lines 12 through 17 by
          R(J,K)=Y1+DEL1R*X1-SUCO-DEL0*X1*Y1
          Z(J,K)=Y2+DEL1Z*X2+SUSI-DEL0*X1*Y2
          RU(J,K)=(-Y2+SUSIU+DEL0*X1*Y2)*UBARP
          ZU(J,K)=(Y1+SUCOU-DEL0*X1*Y1)*UBARP
          RV(J,K)=PI2*(-DEL1R*X2-SUSIV+DEL0*X2*Y1)+UBARPV*(-Y2+SUSIU+DEL0*X1
         1*Y2)
          ZV(J,K)=PI2*(DEL1Z*X1-SUCOV+DEL0*X2*Y2)+UBARPV*(Y1+SUCOU-DEL0*X1*
```

1Y1)

Page 188, for NGEOM = 5 insert after line 18
```
101 CONTINUE
    AKV=FLOAT(IROT)/FLOAT(N)
    VS=FLOAT(N)*VP1
    VSV=FLOAT(N)*PI2
    US=UP1+AKV*VS+ALFU*SIN(UP1)
    USS=UP1+(AKV-1.)*VS+ALFU*SIN(UP1)
    USU=PI2*(1.0+ALFU*COS(UP1))
    USV=AKV*VSV
    USSU=PI2*(1.0+ALFU*COS(UP1))
    USSV=(AKV-1.)*VSV
    RS=0.0
    ZS=0.0
    RSU=0.0
    ZSU=0.0
    RSV=0.0
    ZSV=0.0
    DO 102 MM=1,7
    M=MM-3
    XX1=COS((M-1)*USS-VS)*DELMM(MM)
    XX2=SIN((M-1)*USS-VS)*DELMM(MM)
    RS=RS-XX1
    ZS=ZS+XX2
    XX1U=-XX2*(M-1)*USSU
    XX2U=XX1*(M-1)*USSU
    RSU=RSU-XX1U
    ZSU=ZSU+XX2U
    XX1V=-XX2*((M-1)*USSV-VSV)
    XX2V=XX1*((M-1)*USSV-VSV)
    RSV=RSV-XX1V
    ZSV=ZSV+XX2V
102 CONTINUE
    DO 103 MM=1,2
    M=MM+1
    XX1=COS((M-1)*US-VS)*DELM(MM)
    XX2=SIN((M-1)*US-VS)*DELM(MM)
    RS=RS-XX1
    ZS=ZS+XX2
    XX1U=-XX2*((M-1)*USU)
    XX2U=XX1*((M-1)*USU)
    XX1V=-XX2*((M-1)*USV-VSV)
    XX2V=XX1*((M-1)*USV-VSV)
    RSU=RSU-XX1U
    ZSU=ZSU+XX2U
    RSV=RSV-XX1V
    ZSV=ZSV+XX2V
103 CONTINUE
    DO 104 MM=1,2
    M=MM+1
    XX1=COS((M-1)*US)*DELMO(MM)
    XX2=SIN((M-1)*US)*DELMO(MM)
    XX1U=-XX2*(M-1)*USU
    XX2U=XX1*(M-1)*USU
    XX1V=-XX2*(M-1)*USV
    XX2V=XX1*(M-1)*USV
    RS=RS-XX1
    ZS=ZS+XX2
    RSU=RSU-XX1U
    ZSU=ZSU+XX2U
```

```
       RSV=RSV-XX1V
       ZSV=ZSV+XX2V
 104 CONTINUE
       R(J,K)=RS
       Z(J,K)=ZS
       RU(J,K)=RSU
       ZU(J,K)=ZSU
       RV(J,K)=RSV
       ZV(J,K)=ZSV
       GO TO 140

Page 189, insert after line 26
       IF(NT.GT.0) GO TO 250
       IF(IABS(NVAC).LT.30) GO TO 222
       DO 221 K=1,NP5
       V=PI2*(K-2)*HV/NRUN
       DO 221 J=1,N2
       U=PI2*(J-2)*HU
       AR=(MMODE-1.0)*U-NMODE*V
       EF1(J,K)=-COS(AR)
       EF2(J,K)=PI2*SIN(AR)*(MMODE-1.0)
       EF3(J,K)=-PI2*SIN(AR)*NMODE
       EG1(J,K)=SIN(AR)
       EG2(J,K)=PI2*COS(AR)*(MMODE-1.0)
 221 EG3(J,K)=-PI2*COS(AR)*NMODE
       GO TO 250
 222 CONTINUE

Page 189, insert after line 34
       IF(NGEOM.EQ.5) U=U+IROT*V*NRUN
```

3. Variational principle

We wish to extend the equilibrium and stability code to solutions with surfaces which are not nested and to domains which are not starlike. We should also like to enhance resolution while preserving the previous capabilities of the code, including nonlinear stability calculations. Major issues to be addressed are convergence at the magnetic axis, convergence of the iteration procedure to residuals of the order of the roundoff error, and nonuniqueness of the magnetic field representation. As a first step, a code has been developed and implemented in two space dimensions which solves these problems by a method that generalizes to the fully three-dimensional case. A new magnetic field representation allows for solutions with islands, and a spectral representation results in better resolution. The singularity at the magnetic axis has been removed through the requirement of a regular solution there. An iterative procedure has been developed that converges exponentially to the roundoff error limit so the energy can be computed to the seventh or eighth digit of accuracy needed for nonlinear stability calculations.

In our new formulation the topology of the flux surfaces is prescribed by the poloidal flux function, which might in turn be determined from an energy minimization that is analogous to the Dirichlet principle for harmonic functions when $p = 0$. A mapping of physical space onto an auxiliary domain removes the previous starlike limitation of the method and also improves the resolution for complicated configurations. The solution is found by minimization of the energy

$$E = \int (\frac{1}{2} B^2 - p) \, dV \ ,$$

where the magnetic field B is divergence free and the pressure is a given function $p = p(\sigma)$ of the poloidal flux function σ. This form of the variational principle corresponds to setting the gas constant $\gamma = 0$

102

in the standard energy principle [3]. It results in the pressure rather than the mass being the prescribed function of σ for the compressible case. When the flux surfaces are restricted to be nested, it is easy to change the formulation so a mass function is given and to explore the effects of compressibility on stability results.

The representation for the magnetic field, which integrates the equation $\nabla \cdot B = 0$, is taken to be

$$B = \nabla \Psi \times \nabla s + \nabla \sigma \times \nabla v ,$$

where s may be the toroidal flux, σ is the poloidal flux, and v is a measure of the toroidal angle [10,23]. Both s and σ are single-valued functions, while v and Ψ have unit periods in the toroidal and poloidal angles, respectively. We restrict σ to be a function $\sigma = \sigma(s,\Psi)$ of s and Ψ, so that it is a flux satisfying $B \cdot \nabla \sigma = 0$. Since $p = p(\sigma)$ it follows that $B \cdot \nabla p = 0$, too. The poloidal flux function σ is given and it satisfies the boundary conditions

$$\sigma(0,\Psi) = 0 , \quad \sigma(1,\Psi) = \sigma_0 ,$$

where s = 0 at the magnetic axis and s = 1 at the plasma surface. The dependence of σ on Ψ determines the topology of the flux surfaces, with $\sigma = \sigma(s)$ in the nested case. Note that in general s is no longer a flux function and $B \cdot \nabla s \neq 0$.

Let A+r, θ, z be a modified cylindrical coordinate system, where A is the major radius of the torus and θ is the toroidal angle. We look for a mapping to coordinates s, u, v, where s is a measure of distance from the magnetic axis, while u and v are poloidal and toroidal angles, respectively. We are free to choose v to satisfy

$$\theta = v/A$$

with $0 \leq v \leq L = 2\pi A$ and $0 \leq u \leq 1$. The periodicity conditions imposed on Ψ are

$$\Psi(s,u+1,v) = \Psi(s,u,v) + 1.0 \ ,$$

$$\Psi(s,u,v+L) = \Psi(s,u,v) \ .$$

Let the plasma be the image under a mapping

$$r = r(\tilde{r},\tilde{z}) \ , \quad z = z(\tilde{r},\tilde{z})$$

of a region in some parameter space with coordinates $\tilde{r}$, θ, $\tilde{z}$, and put

$$\tilde{r} = r_0(v) + R(s,u,v) \ [r_1(u,v) - r_0(v)] \ ,$$

$$\tilde{z} = z_0(v) + R(s,u,v) \ [z_1(u,v) - z_0(v)] \ .$$

The radial function R is supposed to satisfy the boundary conditions

$$R(0,u,v) = 0 \ , \quad R(1,u,v) = 1 \ ,$$

and we assume that $0 < R_s < \infty$, which implies that the Jacobian is positive and bounded.   The terms r_0 and z_0 define the magnetic axis, whereas the terms r_1 and z_1 define the plasma boundary. The mapping can be chosen to provide a coordinate system with good zoning that works for flux surfaces that are not starlike in physical space.

Let $\epsilon = 1/A$ be the inverse aspect ratio, $L = 2\pi A$ be the length of the torus, and put $K = 1+\epsilon r$. Assume axial symmetry, so that r, z, and σ are independent of v. The magnetic field components are given by

$$B_r = \frac{1}{KD} \frac{\partial(\sigma,r)}{\partial(s,u)} \ , \quad B_\theta = \frac{\Psi_u}{D} \ , \quad B_z = \frac{1}{KD} \frac{\partial(\sigma,z)}{\partial(s,u)} \ ,$$

where

$$D = \frac{\partial(r,z)}{\partial(s,u)} \ , \quad KD = \frac{\partial(x,y,z)}{\partial(s,v,u)}$$

are Jacobians of the transformation.

104

In the (s,u)-plane we consider the energy functional $E = E(R,\Psi)$. If its first variation is given by

$$\delta E = - L \int_0^1 \int_0^1 [L_1(\Psi)\ \delta\Psi + L_2(R)\ \delta R]\ ds\ du\ ,$$

then after integration by parts the Euler equations can be written as

$$L_1(\Psi) = \frac{\partial}{\partial u}\ (KB_\theta) + \sigma_\Psi L_3(\sigma) = 0\ ,$$

$$L_2(R) = -\frac{1}{R_s}\ [\sigma_s L_3(\sigma) + \Psi_u(KB_\theta)_s] = 0\ .$$

It is important to keep the equations in conservation form so they can serve to define weak solutions. Here the operator $L_3(\sigma)$ is defined by

$$L_3(\sigma) = (B_r r_u + B_z z_u)_s - (B_r r_s + B_z z_s)_u + p'(\sigma)\ KD\ .$$

The Euler equations are equivalent to the equations

$$J \times B = \nabla p\ ,\quad J = \nabla \times B$$

for magnetohydrodynamic equilibrium.

At the magnetic axis $\nabla s = 0$, and assuming s to be regular there we have

$$s = A_{11}(r-r_0)^2 + 2A_{12}(r-r_0)(z-z_0) + A_{22}(z-z_0)^2 + O(s^{3/2})\ .$$

After differentiation with respect to s and renormalization at $s = 0$ we obtain

$$\frac{1}{(R^2)_s} = A_{11}f_1(u)^2 + 2A_{12}f_1(u)\ f_2(u) + A_{22}f_2(u)^2\ ,$$

where

$$f_1(u) = (r_1-r_0)\ \frac{\partial r}{\partial \tilde{r}} + (z_1-z_0)\ \frac{\partial r}{\partial \tilde{z}}\ ,$$

105

$$f_2(u) = (r_1 - r_0) \frac{\partial z}{\partial \tilde{r}} + (z_1 - z_0) \frac{\partial z}{\partial \tilde{z}} .$$

It is not convenient to impose this representation on R_s directly at $s = 0$ because that requires a higher order method. But the equation for Ψ at the axis reduces to

$$\frac{\partial}{\partial u} \left(\frac{\Psi_u}{D} \right) = 0 ,$$

since $\sigma_\Psi = 0$ there. It can be integrated to yield

$$\Psi_u = f_0 D = f_0 H(u) R_s^2 , \qquad H(u) = (r_1 - r_0)(z_1)_u - (z_1 - z_0)(r_1)_u.$$

Then Ψ_u on the axis can be represented in the form

$$\Psi_u = \frac{\tilde{\Psi}_u}{\int_0^1 \tilde{\Psi}_u \, du} , \qquad \tilde{\Psi}_u = \frac{f_0 H(u)}{A_{11} f_1(u)^2 + 2A_{12} f_1(u) f_2(u) + A_{22} f_2(u)^2} .$$

From this we obtain equations for A_{11}, A_{12}, A_{22}, r_0, z_0 by minimizing the energy. The resulting equations amount to setting the first few moments of the toroidal field B_θ equal to zero. They determine the magnetic axis position as well as the elliptical shape of the flux surfaces in the neighborhood of the axis. The accuracy is improved over that in the published BETA code [4], which uses R rather than Ψ to implement the minimization with respect to A_{11}, A_{12} and A_{22}.

4. The spectral method

There is a wide range of problems in computational physics which can be solved efficiently using spectral methods, and applications to the magnetohydrodynamic equilibrium and stability problem are discussed by Hender, Carreras et al. [17], Hirshman and Hogan [19], and Schwenn [29]. The most relevant requirement for these methods is that the solution have periodicity properties. The equilibrium problem in a torus is suitable for a spectral representation in the poloidal and toroidal angles that suggests it as a candidate.

The nonlinear character of the problem and the complicated form of the partial differential equations resulting from an inverse formulation make it difficult to use direct convolutions to evaluate the spectral equations. Therefore we use a collocation method in which the equations are evaluated at prescribed points. While all u derivatives are calculated from the spectral representation, products and quotients are done directly in (s,u)-space.

Let us consider the representations

$$R(s,u) = \sum_{|m| \leq MF} R_m(s)\, e^{2\pi imu} , \qquad R_m(0) = 0, \quad R_0(1) = 1, \quad R_m(1) = 0,$$

$$\Psi(s,u) = u + \sum_{|m| \leq MF} \Psi_m(s)\, e^{2\pi imu} ,$$

$$\sigma(s,\Psi) = \sum_{|m| \leq MF} \sigma_m(s)\, e^{2\pi im\Psi} , \quad \sigma_m(0) = 0, \quad \sigma_0(1) = \sigma_0, \quad \sigma_m(1) = 0 .$$

Collocation points are chosen equally distributed in u,

$$u_j = (j-1)h_u , \quad j = 1,\ldots,NJ, \quad h_u = 1/NJ ,$$

and in the radial direction we put

$$s_i = [(i-1)h_r]^{(1+\alpha)/2} , \quad i = 1,\ldots,NI+1, \quad h_r = 1/NI ,$$

where α controls the radial mesh scaling. The differential equations are then evaluated at the collocation points. This involves the components of B and the derivatives of the mapping $r = r(s,u)$, $z = z(s,u)$, all of which are evaluated at midpoints in the radial direction.

Let $<f>$ denote the value of f at midpoints. When f behaves like $\sqrt{s}$ or $1/\sqrt{s}$ in the neighborhood of the magnetic axis, i.e. for small s, we define

$$<f> = <\sqrt{s}\ f> / <\sqrt{s}> .$$

107

Similarly, if f behaves like $\sqrt{s}$ we approximate the derivative f_s at the midpoint between s_{i+1} and s_i by

$$<f_s> = \frac{1}{2\sqrt{<s>}} \frac{f_{i+1} - f_i}{\sqrt{s_{i+1}} - \sqrt{s_i}} \;.$$

But if f behaves like s near the axis, the usual average and centered differences are used.

A more fundamental question is the choice of radial collocation points for the unknowns R and Ψ. The values of R are taken at the points s_i described above, which include s = 0 and s = 1, where boundary conditions are satisfied. We can choose the same collocation points for Ψ, or we can evaluate Ψ at midpoints between the collocation points of R. We call the latter choice the centered option. It is admissible because Ψ does not satisfy any boundary conditions in s, but only periodicity conditions in u. Furthermore, in the nested case $\sigma = \sigma(s)$ only tangential derivatives of Ψ appear. As a result, the equations for Ψ are decoupled and can be solved at each s in terms of the adjacent values of R. This in turn leads to a three point formula for the R equation which is able to capture sharp discontinuities in the solution due to current sheets at resonances (cf. Section 5).

In the usual option which is not centered, the solution of the Ψ equation is coupled to the values of R at s_{i+1} and s_{i-1}, which in turn are coupled to values at s_{i+2} and s_{i-2}, and so on. As a result the discrete equations are not able to capture a sharp discontinuity accurately, and resonances become smeared. On the other hand, a code that is truly sensitive to the resonances will invariably encounter them in the three-dimensional case and may experience difficulties [9]. In particular, the iterative procedure does not converge unless specific provisions have been made to deal with resonance. These might include truncation of the Fourier series to avoid resonances or addition of a small artificial viscosity term to the R equation. The latter approach may be implemented by using equations that are not centered, which

108

excludes the effect of resonances through truncation error and makes the method always converge. Then resonances can be studied by modifying the flux function σ so as to allow islands to form while avoiding the formation of current sheets. It remains to be seen whether this will succeed in three dimensions, where the problem becomes harder because of subtle existence questions.

For an iterative scheme, we compute the Fourier coefficients of the differential operators

$$L_1(\Psi) = \sum_{|m| \leq MF} \ell_{1m}(s) \, e^{2\pi i m u} \; ,$$

$$L_2(R) = \sum_{|m| \leq MF} \ell_{2m}(s) \, e^{2\pi i m u} \; .$$

Then we write

$$\delta E = -L \iint [L_1(\Psi) \; \delta\Psi + L_2(R) \; \delta R] \; ds \; du$$

$$= -L \sum_m \int (\ell_{1m} \; \delta\Psi_m + \ell_{2m} \; \delta R_m) \; ds$$

and define accelerated paths of steepest descent given by the differential equations

$$(\Psi_m)_{tt} + e_0(\Psi_m)_t = \ell_{1m}/(a_1 \; \min[1,m^2]) \; ,$$

$$(R_m)_{tt} + e_0(R_m)_t = \ell_{2m}/(a_2 \; \min[1,m^2]) \; .$$

The right-hand sides have been scaled using the mode number m, and the descent coefficient e_0 is determined from the iteration itself by estimating the dominant eigenvalue [3]. Faster convergence has been obtained than with earlier versions of the method.

Computational results from a preliminary two-dimensional code show that in general we are able to use the iterative method just described to solve the spectral equations without the convergence deteriorating at any level, so we can determine the discrete solution to as many significant figures as may be required. As a result, the question of accuracy only depends on extrapolation rules for the radial mesh size and on the error introduced by truncation of the Fourier series.

In the presence of a large resonance, which can be introduced in the two-dimensional case by choosing a rotational transform that goes through zero, the code converges at every mesh. An island is detected when the topology of the flux function σ is modified. However, a centered version of the code does not converge so well, and a sharp current sheet appears at the resonant surface. In this case the Jacobian of our transformation of coordinates approaches zero at the resonant surface, which partly accounts for the convergence difficulties. Similar behavior may be expected in three dimensions when resonant surfaces are present inside the plasma.

We study accuracy and extrapolation rules by comparing our results with an exact axisymmetric equilibrium [3]. The boundary of the plasma we choose is roughly elliptical, with an inverse aspect ratio $\epsilon = 0.25$. The pressure is given by $p(\sigma) = 0.125 (1-\sigma)$, the rotational transform is

$$\iota(\sigma) = 2[\frac{4-\sigma}{10-\sigma}]^{1/2} ,$$

and the poloidal flux function is

$$\sigma(r,z) = \frac{2}{5} z^2 + \frac{1}{64} [(r+4)^2 - 16]^2 .$$

For these parameters, the magnetic axis is located at $r_0 = 0.0$ and the energy $E = 61.20852488$.

Fig. 28 shows the extrapolation for the magnetic axis location. We vary the radial mesh scaling α, with $\alpha = 0$ corresponding to a mesh with spacing proportional to toroidal flux and $\alpha = 1$ corresponding to a mesh with spacing proportional to distance from the axis. The extrapolation rules are

$$r_0 = A_0 + A_1 h + A_2 h^2$$

for the magnetic axis and

$$E = A_0 + A_2 h^2 + A_3 h^3$$

110

for the energy, where h is the radial mesh spacing and the number of Fourier components MF has been held fixed. Table 3 shows the extrapolated results for various numbers MF of Fourier components and numbers NJ of collocation points in the poloidal angle. Identical numbers of radial mesh points were used in each case.

MF	NJ	r_0	E
4	16	0.000708	61.2088147
6	24	0.000138	61.2085253
8	32	0.000072	61.20852158
12	48	0.000072	61.20852154

Table 3. Convergence of the spectral method with spacing parameter $\alpha = 1$.

In this problem it seems that eight Fourier components are adequate, but if we want smaller error we need to include a larger number of radial mesh points. A comparable study with $\alpha = 0$ (flux scaling) yields for MF = 6 and NJ = 24 the values $r_0 = 0.0014$ and E = 61.20852485. As expected, the axis error is larger because of the larger spacing in the neighborhood of s = 0, but the energy is very accurate.

For a centered version of the code, the axis location is extremely accurate even at fairly crude meshes. With only 16 radial points, its error is less than 10^{-5}. The error in the energy is also smaller by a factor of three. The convergence, however, is slower, and as we have already mentioned, a special treatment of resonant cases is required.

The next example shows the merit of conformal mapping to handle a bean-shaped cross section that is not starlike. Fig. 29 displays the resulting mesh in the physical (r,z)-plane, but the level curves of σ

become convex in the plane of the parameters $\tilde{r}$ and $\tilde{z}$. The conformal mapping is given by

$$w(\varsigma) = \varsigma \sqrt{\varsigma^2 + 1} + \varsigma^2 ,$$

where $\varsigma = \tilde{r} + i\tilde{z}$ and $w = r + iz$. The mapping concentrates mesh points in the region of high curvature and it allows us to describe the solution with a small number of Fourier coefficients.

The last example involves a solution with flux surfaces that are not nested. The topology of the surfaces depends on the flux function σ, and they are shown in Fig. 30. Here σ is prescribed to be

$$\sigma = \sigma_0(s) + \sigma_3(s) \cos 3\Psi_3 ,$$

with $\sigma_0'(s)$ changing sign at the resonant surface $s = 0.6$. We can also compute $\sigma_3(s)$ by minimizing the functional E with $\sigma_0(s)$ held fixed, in which case the island width is determined from the minimization itself. Convergence of the artificial time iteration is good.

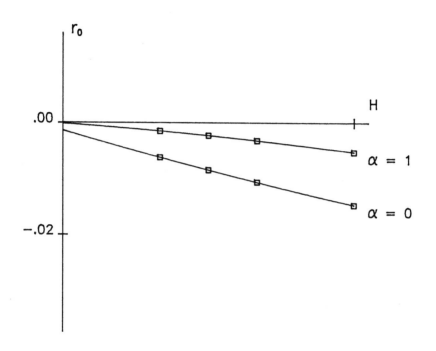

Fig. 28. Convergence study of the shift r_0 of the magnetic axis calculated by the noncentered spectral code in two dimensions for various mesh sizes h and mesh scalings α with MF = 6. For a centered version of the code the error becomes less than 10^{-5} using only 16 radial points.

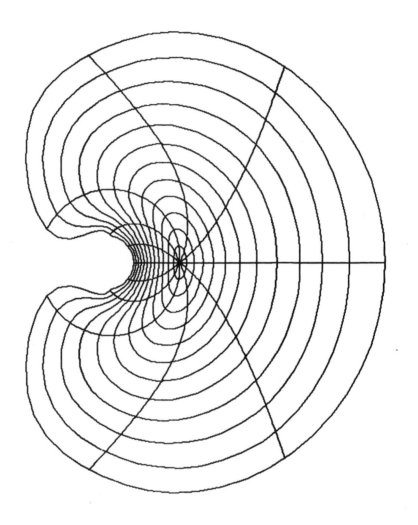

Fig. 29. Calculation of equilibrium based on a coordinate transformation that lifts the restriction to starlike flux surfaces.

Fig. 30. Equilibrium with three islands calculated in two dimensions using a formulation of the variational principle based on a representation of the magnetic field as the sum of two cross products.

5. Asymptotic convergence to a weak solution

In this section we shall discuss questions about the existence and regularity of solutions of the partial differential equations for ideal magnetohydrodynamic equilibrium in three dimensions. The numerical method implemented in the BETA code uses the toroidal flux s as an independent variable, which entails the hypothesis that the magnetic surfaces s = const. are a nested family of tori. In cases without two-dimensional symmetry the KAM theory of dynamical systems shows that smooth solutions with nested surfaces do not in general exist [15]. However, the finite difference scheme in the code leads to a construction of weak solutions because the partial differential equations are expressed in conservation form. The meaning of a weak solution will be defined, and its relationship to current sheets will be explained. The theory suggests that the numerical method converges in an asymptotic sense and furnishes an accurate model of the salient features of stellarator physics for small mesh size h > 0. A critical comparison will be made of the finite difference approach presently used in three dimensions with the spectral representation whose advantages have been described in the previous section for equilibria in two dimensions.

The KAM theorem gives conditions under which perturbations of an equilibrium with nested flux surfaces will still have a dense family of good surfaces, even though they may be intermingled with islands and ergodic regions [22]. The principal requirement is that the shear $\iota' = \iota'(s)$ differ from zero. This favorable property of shear is reflected in recent results from the Wendelstein VII-A experiment, which shows dramatic improvement in confinement even when only a small amount of shear is introduced. More subtle aspects of the KAM theory have been used to demonstrate the nonexistence of smooth equilibria in three dimensions [15]. We shall give a simplified version of the proof that

116

emerges naturally from formulas underlying the BETA equilibrium, stability and transport codes.

In our model the magnetic field

$$B = \nabla s \times \nabla \psi = \nabla \phi + \zeta \nabla s$$

.s represented in terms of two flux functions s and ψ and two Clebsch potentials ϕ and ζ. To evaluate the Mercier local stability criterion $\Omega > 0$ or to calculate transport coefficients what is required is the Fourier series

$$\frac{1}{B^2} = \sum b_{mn}(s) \cos(m\psi + [n-\iota m]\phi) \quad,$$

which is computed reliably by the equilibrium code. Taking the divergence of the cross product of the magnetostatic equations $J \times B = \nabla p$ with B/B^2, one deduces the formula

$$\frac{\partial \lambda}{\partial \phi} = \frac{\partial}{\partial \psi} \frac{1}{B^2}$$

relating $1/B^2$ to the renormalized Pfirsch-Schlueter current

$$\lambda = \frac{J \cdot B}{p'(s)B^2} \quad .$$

This is a linear partial differential equation of the first order that can be integrated formally to derive for λ the Fourier representation

$$\lambda = \sum \frac{m b_{mn}}{n - \iota m} \cos(m\psi + [n-\iota m]\phi) \quad .$$

If λ is well behaved it becomes apparent that the coefficient $b_{mn} = b_{mn}(s)$ must vanish on any rational surface s = const. where $\iota = n/m$. This is the crux of the nonexistence proof. In practice numerical computation of low order resonant coefficients b_{mn} provides a diagnostic for the presence of islands in the equilibrium. Similarly, a negative

117

result $\Omega < 0$ for the Mercier criterion associated with large values of λ has been interpreted as an indication that pressure gradients are producing islands, although there may also be some correlation with resistive magnetohydrodynamic activity.

Two-dimensional versions of the BETA equilibrium code have been used to show that when islands ought to be present in the solution, current sheets appear instead. This is because the magnetostatic equations have been coded in a conservation form admitting weak solutions that need not be continuous [3]. Let us introduce the Maxwell stress tensor

$$T_{ij} = B_i B_j - \delta_{ij} (\frac{1}{2} B^2 + p) ,$$

where B_i stands for the ith component of the magnetic field B and δ_{ij} is the Kronecker delta. The conservation, or divergence, form of the equilibrium equations is

$$\sum \frac{\partial B_i}{\partial x_i} = 0 , \qquad \sum \frac{\partial T_{ij}}{\partial x_i} = 0 , \qquad j = 1,2,3.$$

Multiplying by test functions g and g_j of compact support, integrating and applying the divergence theorem, we obtain

$$\iiint \sum B_i \frac{\partial g}{\partial x_i} \, dx_1 \, dx_2 \, dx_3 = 0 ,$$

$$\iiint \sum T_{ij} \frac{\partial g_j}{\partial x_i} \, dx_1 \, dx_2 \, dx_3 = 0 , \qquad j = 1,2,3.$$

We say that the field components B_i and the pressure p are a weak solution of the magnetostatic equations if they are bounded measurable functions fulfilling these four identities for all smooth test functions g and g_j of appropriate compact support. No differentiability of B_i and p is assumed, and no information is sought about fine structure of the equilibrium. If a surface of discontinuity is present in an otherwise smooth weak solution of the equilibrium equations, then it can be shown to be a flux surface satisfying the jump condition for a current sheet, which asserts that $B^2/2 + p$ remains continuous.

The finite difference equations implemented in the BETA equilibrium code are in conservation form with respect to a system of modified flux coordinates (cf. Section 3). It is for this reason that we expect the numerical solution to converge in some sense to a weak solution. There is an analogy here with the Euler equations for steady flow, where a related theory of shock waves has become widely accepted [21]. The problem of capturing shock waves is in a way harder because it involves an entropy inequality, usually modeled by low order numerical viscosity, that plays no role for vortex sheets, which are the equivalent of our current sheets. In plasma physics the effect of a finite gyroradius is much larger than the viscosity occurring in most problems of fluid dynamics. It is closer to the high order artificial viscosity due to truncation errors in the BETA code. Current sheets become thoroughly smeared in both physical and computational data for stellarators. Therefore we presume that the convergence of our numerical method is adequate in the asymptotic sense that optimal results are obtained for a small but positive choice of the mesh size h. A more detailed analysis showing just how a weak solution emerges in the limit as h → 0 is of less practical interest.

The conservation form of the difference equations in the BETA code follows naturally from an application of the finite element method to the variational principle of ideal magnetohydrodynamics, with an ergodic constraint p = p(s) imposed on the pressure [3]. This leads to the construction of a weak solution of the equilibrium equations that does not violate the nested surface hypothesis. It will be interesting to see whether the spectral method meets with comparable success. Finite difference schemes in conservation form capture discontinuities quite effectively, whereas jumps such as occur across a current sheet might trigger the Gibbs phenomenon in a Fourier series. That could cause difficulties with convergence, and resonances may be hard to control in a procedure requiring decisions to be made about which harmonics to include in the approximation. However, there is evidence that the rotational transform and shift of the magnetic axis can be determined with ease by the spectral method for configurations that are not too complicated [29], and a judicious addition of artificial viscosity seems to help.

Severe symptoms of nonexistence are surely to be avoided in the design of stellarators. Numerical experiments with line tracing in vacuum fields suggest that this is not hard to accomplish in practice [25]. Resonant coefficients b_{mn} in the Fourier expansion of $1/B^2$ must be monitored and if possible reduced. Small deviations from the Mercier criterion $\Omega > 0$ do not seem to have been fatal for the Heliotron E experiment, but the same cannot be promised for major violations. Although nonlinear stability may be the primary test for a β limit, both local criteria and transport must be given careful consideration, too. The purpose of the BETA equilibrium, stability and transport codes is to make available a computational tool with which to assess all these issues.

IV. NEOCLASSICAL TRANSPORT

1. The Monte Carlo method

In the BETA transport code a simplified computational model of
plasma confinement is implemented that couples a linearized drift
kinetic equation for the distribution of ions or electrons to a magnetic
field defined by ideal magnetohydrodynamic equilibrium. This is not
altogether self-consistent, but seems to work well anyway. No attempt
is made to allow particle motion to influence the magnetic field, which
is calculated once and for all by means of the BETA equilibrium code. A
plausible temperature profile $T = T(s)$ is imposed at the outset, so
particle confinement times rather than energy confinement times are
computed. The drift kinetic equation is analyzed numerically by a fast
version of the Monte Carlo method of Boozer and Kuo-Petravic [12] that
enables one to handle electrons as well as ions in practice. A new
feature of the model is a self-consistent determination of the electric
field from a quasineutrality requirement on the distribution functions
for the two species. A principal conclusion from the theory is that
there will be a loss of confinement through the electron channel if the
computed confinement time τ_e for the electrons turns out to be
significantly smaller than the corresponding ion confinement time τ_i for
all reasonable choices of the electric potential Φ, which need not be a
function of toroidal magnetic flux s alone. The code can be used to
look for such a possiblity.

The linearized drift kinetic equation for the distribution f of
ions or electrons has the form

$$f_t + \rho_\parallel [B + \nabla \times (\rho_\parallel B)] \cdot \nabla f = \nabla \cdot (\nu\, e^{-Mv^2/2T} \nabla e^{Mv^2/2T} f) \ ,$$

where the operator ∇ refers to differentiation with respect to space coordinates on the left but with respect to velocity coordinates on the right. The magnetic field

$$B = \nabla s \times \nabla \psi = \nabla \phi + \zeta \nabla s$$

is specified in terms of the toroidal flux s, a multiple-valued poloidal flux variable ψ, and a Clebsch potential ϕ by a run of the BETA equilibrium code. All that is required to trace guiding center orbits, which follow the drift velocity shown in square brackets, is a knowledge of the Fourier series

$$\frac{1}{B^2} = \sum b_{mn}(s) \cos(m\psi + [n-\iota m]\phi) ,$$

where $\iota = \iota(s)$ is the rotational transform. Because B^2 is the Jacobian of the renormalized variables s, ψ and ϕ with respect to physical coordinates, the Fourier coefficients b_{mn} are computed reliably as double integrals

$$b_{mn} = \iint D \cos(m\psi + [n-\iota m]\phi) \, du \, dv$$

over the nested flux surfaces s = const. of a further Jacobian D, where u and v are poloidal and toroidal angles occurring in the equilibrium code. This procedure is quite different from what is usually done when B is given by the Biot-Savart formula for vacuum fields [14].

The parallel gyroradius $\rho_\parallel$ is defined by the energy conservation law

$$W = \frac{1}{2M} \rho_\parallel^2 + \mu B + q\Phi ,$$

where W is a constant, M is the particle mass, μ is the magnetic moment, and q is the charge. The electric potential Φ is allowed to depend on ψ and ϕ as well as s in the system of ordinary differential equations for the guiding center orbits, which include an equation for $\rho_\parallel$ so as to uniformize the turning points of trapped particles. A constant value of the collision frequency ν is assumed in the Fokker-Planck operator on the right-hand side of the drift kinetic equation. Extensive numerical

122

experiments suggest that neoclassical transport is relatively insensitive to details in the form of the collision operator, so we have used a simple second order partial differential operator having the Maxwellian $\exp(-Mv^2/2T)$ as a particular solution. Essentially all that matters is the choice of the two coefficients T and ν.

The drift kinetic equation is solved numerically by a Monte Carlo method in which many orbits are traced by alternating systematically between integrations of the guiding center equations and applications of a random walk that models the collision operator [5]. The distribution function f is found to decay exponentially, so we put

$$f = F\, e^{-t/\tau} \ ,$$

where F is supposed to become independent of the time t, and τ is the particle confinement time. Substitution back into the drift kinetic equation leads in the limit as $t \to \infty$ to a relation

$$\rho_{\|}[B + \nabla \times (\rho_{\|}B)]\cdot\nabla F = \nabla\cdot(\nu\, e^{-Mv^2/2T}\, \nabla\, e^{Mv^2/2T}\, F) + F/\tau$$

for F in which t disappears. If the last term on the right is interpreted as a source $S = F/\tau$, we arrive at the suggestive representation

$$\tau = \frac{\|F\|}{\|S\|}$$

of the confinement time using any reasonable definition of the norm.

To calculate τ numerically we monitor the exponential decay of various integrals of f. For example, an expected value of the form

$$\Gamma = \sum\sum \cos(\frac{s_{jk}-\sigma_k}{1-\sigma_k s_{jk}}\, \frac{\pi}{2}) \simeq A\, e^{-t/\tau} \ ,$$

where s_{jk} stands for the radial coordinate s of the jth particle launched from the nested surface $s = \sigma_k$, provides good estimates of τ for both ions and electrons. In a similar way the Fourier coefficients

$$F_{mn} = \iint <F> \cos(m\psi + [n-\iota m]\phi)\ d\psi\ d\phi$$

of the stationary distribution function $<F>$ averaged over velocity space are evaluated by monitoring expected values of appropriate trigonometric functions of the flux coordinates of the particles. Satisfactory values of τ and of low order coefficients F_{mn} for ions can be obtained by following several hundred orbits for roughly half the escape time. In practical cases this takes about 30 minutes on the Cray X-MP/48 computer at the San Diego Supercomputer Center. A comparable result for electrons may require a two hour run. The latter calculation is accomplished efficiently because it is only necessary to examine the expected value Γ over a relatively short interval of time.

To complete our model of confinement it becomes necessary to formulate self-consistent conditions determining the electric potential Φ. For that purpose let us consider Poisson's equation

$$\frac{1}{c^2} \Delta\Phi = <F_i> - <F_e>,$$

where $<F_i>$ and $<F_e>$ represent the averages over velocity space of stationary distributions of ions and electrons associated with a given configuration. Because of the size of the speed of light c, it turns out that several significant figures in the values of $<F_i>$ and $<F_e>$ must coincide unless the electric field is to become unreasonably large. Therefore we impose the quasineutrality requirement

$$<F_i> = <F_e>$$

124

as an appropriate equation to solve for Φ, together with the ambipolarity condition

$$\tau_i = \tau_e$$

asserting that the ion and electron confinement times τ_i and τ_e are equal.

It is more customary in the literature [12,14,32] to find Φ from Ohm's law, which we prefer to write in a form

$$E + U \times B = \eta_1 J - \frac{B}{B^2} \nabla \cdot (\eta_2 \nabla \frac{J \cdot B}{B^2})$$

introduced recently [11]. Here E is the electric field, U is the diffusive flow vector, J is the current density, η_1 is the Spitzer resistivity, and η_2 is a coefficient modeling the effect of turbulence. Since the component of E parallel to B is small, it is reasonable to suppose that

$$\Phi = \Phi(s, \psi)$$

is constant along the lines of force and consequently depends on just the flux functions s and ψ. Because ψ is multiple-valued and the lines of force are ergodic on any toroidal flux surface s = const. where the rotational transform ι is irrational, it is usually assumed that Φ is a function of s alone. However, that conclusion is based on a somewhat singular integration of the partial differential equation

$$B \cdot \nabla \Phi = 0 \ ,$$

in which the right-hand side may not actually vanish when η_1 and η_2 differ from zero. This phenomenon is especially pronounced at rational surfaces where $\iota = n/m$ with low values of the integers m and n. Hence it is plausible that Φ depends on all three of the coordinates s, ψ and

125

ϕ, especially if ψ and ϕ occur in the resonant combination $m\psi + [n - \iota m]\phi$, which varies little along the lines of force. Thus we prefer quasineutrality to Ohm's law as an equation for Φ. It is unreasonable to impose both.

With these considerations in mind, we express the electric potential Φ as a Fourier series

$$\Phi = P_{00}(1-s) + \sum P_{mn} \cos(m\psi + [n - \iota m]\phi)$$

in the poloidal and toroidal variables ψ and ϕ, with coefficients $P_{mn} = P_{mn}(s)$ depending on the toroidal flux s. Representing the charge separation

$$<F_i> - <F_e> = \sum C_{mn} \cos(m\psi + [n - \iota m]\phi)$$

in a similar fashion, we calculate low order Fourier coefficients C_{mn} and drive them toward zero in a discrete approximation to the quasineutrality requirement $<F_i> = <F_e>$. Together with the ambipolarity relation $\tau_i = \tau_e$, this provides an effective spectral method for the computation of the low order Fourier coefficients P_{mn} of Φ.

An iterative procedure to solve for P_{mn} is implemented in practice through repeated runs of the BETA transport code. It works fairly well if only one significant figure is sought in the answer for τ_e/τ_i and for a few coefficients P_{mn}. The relationship between the matrices P_{mn} and C_{mn} is found to be more or less diagonally dominant, but the radial term $P_{00}(1-s)$ has a more complicated dependence on the ratio of confinement times τ_e/τ_i. In Table 4 we display results from a sequence of runs for the TJ-II Heliac experiment that illustrate how a root of the quasineutrality equations may be found by exhaustive but systematic computation following the guidelines we have presented. In this example no attempt was made to take into account the dependence of the coefficients P_{mn} and C_{mn} on s. Successful treatment of the electrons here increases confidence in more standard ion calculations.

A radial coefficient P_{00} in the electric potential Φ of the same order of magnitude as the temperature T tends to detrap the ions and raise their confinement time τ_i significantly while leaving the electron confinement time τ_e almost unchanged. Numerical calculations show that resonant coefficients P_{mn} with $\iota = n/m$ inside the plasma may have the opposite effect of reducing τ_e much more than τ_i even when they are two orders of magnitude smaller than T. Table 2 in Section II.14 provides evidence of this contention about resonance for the TJ-II Heliac. The phenomenon becomes visible at higher collision frequencies ν for which τ_e exceeds τ_i by a factor comparable to the square root of the ratio of the mass M_i of the ions to the mass M_e of the electrons. It leads us to consider the possibility that relatively small terms in Φ that depend on the poloidal and toroidal variables ψ and ϕ may serve in our simplified model of plasma confinement to explain the anomalous transport of electrons that is observed experimentally. Perhaps a self-consistent electric field simulates the effect of drift waves and microinstabilities.

For small values of the gyroradius ρ_L let us introduce drift surfaces $\sigma = $ const. defined by the first order partial differential equation

$$[B + \nabla \times (\rho_\parallel B)] \cdot \nabla \sigma = 0 .$$

We put

$$\sigma = s + \lambda_\parallel ,$$

where $\lambda_\parallel$ is a guiding center step size proportional to the gyroradius ρ_L. Making use of the fact that $B \cdot \nabla s = 0$ and keeping only terms of the order ρ_L in the equation for σ, we obtain after some manipulation the more transparent equation

$$\frac{\partial \lambda_\parallel}{\partial \phi} = \frac{\partial \rho_\parallel}{\partial \psi}$$

127

for $\lambda_\|$. If $\rho_\|$ is suitably expanded in a Fourier series as a function of ψ and ϕ with coefficients ρ_{mn} depending on s, then formal integration of the differential equation for $\lambda_\|$ yields a representation

$$\lambda_\| = \sum \frac{m\rho_{mn}}{n-\iota m} \cos(m\psi + [n-\iota m]\phi)$$

explicitly exhibiting resonance at the rational surfaces. A suitable norm $\|\lambda_\|\|$ of the guiding center step size $\lambda_\|$ is used in the BETA equilibrium code together with a procedure of bounce averaging to compute economically a geometric confinement time [8] that gives a phenomenological measure of neoclassical transport (cf. Fig. 31).

The law of conservation of energy shows that perturbations

$$\delta\Phi = P_{mn} \cos(m\psi + [n-\iota m]\phi)$$

in the electric potential which depend on ψ and ϕ and are much smaller than the temperature T appear in a Taylor expansion of the parallel gyroradius

$$\rho_\| = (2M)^{1/2}[W - \mu B - q\Phi]^{1/2}$$

multiplied by the factor $M^{1/2}$. They contribute to the Fourier series for $\lambda_\|$ terms

$$\delta\lambda_\| = \epsilon m M^{1/2} \, \delta\Phi/4[n-\iota m]$$

that also scale like $M^{1/2}$ but have the small divisors $n-\iota m$.

Clearly $\lambda_\|$ exhibits any resonances that are present in Φ, and for fixed T the islands associated with these resonances may be expected to have widths proportional to $\delta s = M^{1/4}$. This can be seen by resolving the singularity at the rational surface $s = s_0$ where $n = \iota m$ through a modified representation

$$(s-s_0)^2/2 + (s-s_0)\lambda_\| = \text{const.}$$

128

of the drift surfaces, which have a separatrix defined by the asymptotic relation

$$(s-s_0)^2 \sim \frac{\epsilon\, M^{1/2}}{\iota'(s_0)} \sin^2 \frac{m\psi+[n-\iota m]\phi}{2}$$

with island width $\epsilon^{1/2} M^{1/4} \iota'(s_0)^{-1/2}$. Because the collision time is of the order $\delta t = M^{1/2}$, large collections of these islands result in a transport coefficient of the form

$$\frac{1}{\tau} = \frac{\delta s^2}{\delta t} = \frac{M^{2/4}}{M^{1/2}} = 1$$

characterized by the radial step size δs and the time step δt. For ions and electrons of approximately equal temperatures T_i and T_e the perturbation we have described in the electric potential Φ thus provides loss mechanisms of comparable magnitude [13]. If $\tau_e \gg \tau_i$ for $\Phi = 0$ the effect is to lower τ_e much more than τ_i. Combined with a larger radial electric field that improves the confinement of the ions, this could suffice to produce quasineutrality.

Observe that clusters of islands among the magnetic surfaces $s = $ const. have widths δs that are independent of the mass M, so that the resulting transport coefficient $\delta s^2/\delta t$ behaves like $M^{-1/2}$. Since the mass M_e of the electrons is much smaller than the mass M_i of the ions, this means that when the magnetic islands are significant there must be excessive losses through the electron channel. If the islands are caused by a pressure gradient, the losses may account for a soft β limit of the plasma [4]. On the other hand, the islands generated among drift surfaces $\sigma = $ const. by the electric potential Φ presumably just expand until the ambipolarity condition $\tau_i = \tau_e$ and the quasineutrality requirement $\langle F_i \rangle = \langle F_e \rangle$ are met. But when $\tau_e \ll \tau_i$ for all choices of Φ then the electron temperature T_e must drop. Heat conduction becomes important if T_e has to be significantly less than the ion temperature

129

T_i in order to maintain quasineutrality. Such a situation might be expected to prevail as reactor temperatures are approached in stellarators of low aspect ratio with poor confinement due to trapping of the electrons.

The theory we have described has been confirmed in numerical studies of our model made by running the BETA transport code systematically on the Cray X-MP/48 at the San Diego Supercomputer Center (cf. Tables 4 and 5). Repeated runs of the code suffice to determine approximate roots of the equation for quasineutrality if the dimensionless collision frequency $\bar{\nu}$ is not too far from unity. However, in a typical case with $\bar{\nu} \geq 64$ the resolution becomes inadequate because the Fourier coefficients C_{mn} of the charge separation are so small to begin with. In general the runs suggest that a relatively small electric potential serves to bring the confinement time of the electrons down to that of the ions. A radial component of the electric field might raise the latter by a factor of two or three, but the energy confinement time is likely to be two or three times smaller. Stellarators with electron confinement not significantly better than the ion confinement in a reactor regime at zero electric potential are to be avoided because of the more limited possibility of achieving quasineutrality in such cases.

The results we have described seem to agree to a certain extent with recent data from the Heliotron E and Wendelstein VII-A experiments. Thus primary losses through the electron channel have been observed in the Heliotron E at the largest values of β to be achieved. Also pronounced degradation of confinement is known to occur in the Wendelstein VII-A when the rotational transform ι approaches a low order rational number. There is some relevance to experiments in tokamaks, too, for which the divergence term in Ohm's law provides a connection between rapid fluctuations of the magnetic field and our model of equilibrium in three dimensions.

130

The prospects for good transport in a stellarator of low aspect ratio A are doubtful. However, since the major radius of any reactor will have to be very large anyway, there are distinct advantages in considering a virtually two-dimensional solution such as the Heliac with A = 30. The remaining problem is to identify satisfactory specifications for an intermediate stellarator experiment comparable to the TFTR or JET tokamaks that would have acceptable limits on both β and τ for a very hot plasma of moderate aspect ratio and which might be proposed within the framework of present laboratory budgets (cf. Section I.2).

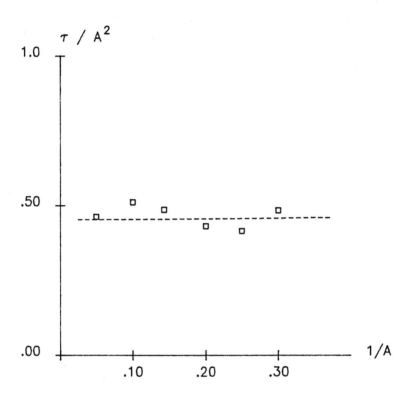

Fig. 31. Graph of the geometric confinement time τ output by the equilibrium code for an $\ell = 2$ stellarator showing that it scales like the square of the aspect ratio A.

P_{00}	P_{01}	P_{13}	P_{11}	P_{10}	τ_i	τ_e	C_{01}	C_{13}	C_{11}	C_{10}
0.0	0.00	0.000	0.00	0.00	12	15	0.11	-.06	0.08	0.05
0.0	-.05	0.000	0.00	0.00	5	150	0.01	0.05	0.05	0.04
0.0	-.05	-.005	0.00	0.00	8	25	0.07	-.03	0.06	0.04
0.0	-.05	-.005	-.03	0.00	5	30	0.01	-.03	0.06	0.05
0.0	-.05	-.005	-.03	-.03	7	40	-.03	-.09	0.01	0.01
-.5	0.00	0.000	0.00	0.00	75	13	-.04	0.02	-.02	0.00
-.5	0.02	0.000	0.00	0.00	95	20	0.01	-.02	-.02	0.00
-.5	0.02	0.005	0.00	0.00	90	10	-.02	-.01	-.05	0.01
-.5	0.02	0.005	0.01	0.00	140	12	-.03	-.04	0.01	0.00
-.1	0.00	0.000	0.00	0.00	12	10	-.11	-.07	-.02	0.00
-.1	0.03	0.000	0.00	0.00	16	9	0.00	-.10	-.01	0.00
-.1	0.03	0.003	0.00	0.00	20	10	0.00	-.02	-.02	-.01

Table 4. Dependence of Fourier coefficients C_{mn} of the charge separation

$$<F_i> - <F_e> = \Sigma\, C_{mn} \cos(m\psi + [n - \iota m]\phi)$$

on corresponding Fourier coefficients P_{mn} of the electric potential

$$\Phi = P_{00}(1-s) + \Sigma\, P_{mn} \cos(m\psi + [n - \iota m]\phi),$$

measured in units of the temperature, for the TJ-II Heliac with ι near 0.3. The ion and electron confinement times τ_i and τ_e are measured in milliseconds for a magnetic field of 1 tesla, and $\bar{\nu} = 4$. In units of the plasma radius, the ion and electron gyroradii are $\rho_i = 0.01$ and $\rho_e = 0.0002$. An approximate root of the quasineutrality equations is observed in the 12th and last row of the table after 11 systematic iterations based on diagonal dominance in the relationship between P_{mn} and C_{mn} have been performed.

P_{00}	P_{10}	P_{11}	τ_i	τ_e	C_{10}	C_{11}
0.0	0.00	0.00	35	7	0.11	-.14
0.0	-.05	0.00	35	12	0.06	-.04
-1.0	0.00	0.00	1200	200	-.08	0.00
-1.0	0.03	0.00	2400	100	0.04	0.02
1.0	0.00	0.00	600	300	0.06	0.06
1.0	-.02	0.00	450	450	0.02	0.05
1.0	-.02	-.02	450	300	0.00	0.03

Table 5. Tentative root of the quasineutrality equations for the TJ-II Heliac with a reversed radial electric field at the low collision frequency $\bar{\nu} = 1/4$.

2. Description of the code

The BETA transport code [5] performs a Monte Carlo calculation of the neoclassical transport of either ions or electrons as described in Section 1. The basic idea is as follows. A particle moves along a guiding center orbit with its energy and magnetic moment held constant. After a time interval related to the collision frequency, the particle suffers a collision which changes its energy E and a parameter η specifying the magnetic moment according to rules which approximate a Fokker-Planck operator. A large collection of particles can be followed for many such time steps. Then exponential decay of functionals of the distribution function f enable one to compute the particle confinement time. This process can be interpreted as a split time numerical solution of the drift kinetic equation for f given in Section 1. In alternate steps we integrate along the characteristics of the first order partial differential operator on the left and then apply a random walk to model the collision operator on the right.

The results from the equilibrium code are in a convenient form for computation of the Fourier coefficients required to follow particle orbits in flux coordinates. The magnetic field is represented by the flux functions s and ψ and the Clebsch potentials ϕ and ς. Tapes 2 and 7 saved from the equilibrium code contain ψ, ϕ and data for the current needed to compute the field in flux coordinates. The orbit equations implemented in the transport code are

$$\frac{ds}{dt} = \mp(\mu+B\rho_\parallel^2)\frac{\partial B}{\partial \psi} - \frac{\partial \Phi}{\partial \psi} \ ,$$

$$\frac{d\psi}{dt} = \pm\,(\mu+B\rho_\parallel^2)(\frac{\partial B}{\partial s} - P_s\varsigma\frac{\partial B}{\partial \phi}) \pm P_s\rho_\parallel^2 + \frac{\partial \Phi}{\partial s} - P_s\varsigma\frac{\partial \Phi}{\partial \phi} \ ,$$

$$\frac{d\phi}{dt} = \pm\,P_s\varsigma(\mu+B\rho_\parallel^2)\frac{\partial B}{\partial \psi} + B^2\rho_\parallel(1\pm P_s\lambda\rho_\parallel) + P_s\varsigma\frac{\partial \Phi}{\partial \psi} \ ,$$

$$\frac{d\rho_\parallel}{dt} = -(\mu+B\rho_\parallel^2)[\frac{\partial B}{\partial \phi} (1\pm p_s\lambda\rho_\parallel) \pm \frac{P_s\rho_\parallel}{B^2} \frac{\partial B}{\partial \psi}] - [\frac{P_s\rho_\parallel}{B^2} \frac{\partial \Phi}{\partial \psi} \pm(1\pm p_s\lambda\rho_\parallel) \frac{\partial \Phi}{\partial \phi}],$$

where the upper sign is used for ions and the lower one for electrons. Additional terms actually appear in the code to allow for net current that is not zero in a tokamak with nontrivial loop voltage. Also, a constraint is imposed to prevent particles from entering a small neighborhood $0 \leq s < s_0$ of the magnetic axis.

The coefficients on the right-hand side of the equations are computed from the equilibrium run. The Fourier coefficients of $1/B^2$ are evaluated and the parallel current is computed from its Fourier series by solving the first order partial differential equations

$$\frac{\partial \lambda}{\partial \phi} = \frac{\partial}{\partial \psi} \frac{1}{B^2},$$
$$\frac{\partial \zeta}{\partial \phi} = \frac{1}{B^2}.$$

The dependence of the coefficients on s is found by using a polynomial to interpolate. Then they are ordered in a sorting routine M01AJF obtained from the NAG Library. The number of coefficients is restricted in the equilibrium code by requiring that $MF \leq NJ/4$ and $NF \leq NK/4$. The number of harmonics is further reduced by means of the input parameter SIZEL, which imposes a limit on the magnitude of the coefficients retained. The ordinary differential equations are integrated numerically using the Adams method available from the NAG Library as D02CHF.

The length of the integration step between collisions is proportional to the input parameter DELT divided by the collision frequency. The dimensionless collision frequency that is a principal input parameter of the code is

$$FREQ = \bar{\nu} = \frac{10^{-18}}{3\nu_R} \frac{\bar{n} \alpha^{1/2}}{BT^{3/2}},$$

where the magnetic field B is measured in tesla, the temperature T is measured in kiloelectron volts, and the density $\bar{n}$ is measured in particles/cm^3. The atomic mass α for ions is 1 for hydrogen and 2 for deuterium. We express $\bar{\nu}$ in terms of a reference collision frequency ν_R = 0.6×10^{-6} which corresponds to the typical reactor values $\bar{n}$ = 2×10^{14} particles/cm^3, T = 10 keV, and B = 5 tesla (cf. [12]). In a typical case we have found that for ions the plateau region is $1 < \bar{\nu} < 1000$.

The number of time steps in a run scales like TEND*SQRT(FREQ)/DELT*SQRT(RADL), where TEND is an input parameter setting the length of the run and

$$RADL = \rho_L = 0.45 \, \frac{T^{1/2}\alpha^{1/2}}{Ba}$$

is the gyroradius for ions measured in units of the plasma radius a, which is given in cm. For equal ion and electron temperatures, the gyroradius RADL of the electrons, which should be input with a minus sign, will be smaller than that of the ions by a factor equal to the square root of the ratio of the ion and electron masses. This has usually been approximated by $64 = 4^3$ for $\alpha = 2$ or by 43 for $\alpha = 1$. It should be noted that the number of time steps also determines the dimension NSTOR required for the variables stored for processing at the end of the run. The array PL(NSTOR,10) is used for this storage and the default value of NSTOR is 7000.

After each completion of the call to the ordinary differential equation solver the code goes to a subroutine where a check is made to see if any particles have been lost. If a loss is detected the number of orbits is readjusted accordingly. The magnetic field, the kinetic energy E, and the magnetic moment parameter $\eta = v_{\parallel}/v$ are then computed using the new values for s, ψ, and ϕ. The functionals used in the computation of the confinement time and the Fourier coefficients of the distribution function needed for our study of the effect of the electric

137

potential on transport are stored. The latter are obtained reliably from expected values of relevant trigonometric functions.

The variation of f due to collisions is represented by the Fokker-Planck collision operator. This is approximated by a random walk in which the velocity of the particle moves at each time step δt with equal probabilities to pairs of neighbors on a discrete mesh of points. The change in η due to a collision is given by

$$\eta_{k+1} = (1 - \nu \, \delta t)\eta_k \pm \sqrt{(1-\eta_k^2)} \, \nu \, \delta t \; ,$$

and similarly the change in E is given by

$$E_{k+1} = E_k \pm 2 \sqrt{TE_k \nu \, \delta t} - 2\nu \, \delta t \, [E_k - (\frac{3}{2} + \frac{E_k}{\nu} \frac{d\nu}{dE_k})T] \; ,$$

where $T = T(s)$ is the temperature and ν is a collision frequency defined in Subroutine COLL. The sign of the radical is chosen with equal probabilities by a random generator RANF on the Cray computer. After that all the data needed to follow the orbits for another time interval between collisions are available and another call to the ordinary differential equation solver is made. Inside the code the temperature distribution T(s) is renormalized so that

$$6 \int_0^1 (1-s) \, T(s) \, ds = \rho_L^2 \; .$$

We need to take a sufficiently large number of particles and follow them for a long enough time in order to develop statistically significant data with which to estimate particle confinement times. We compute confinement times for our samples from exponential decay of functionals of the distribution function. One choice is the expected value

$$\frac{1}{N} \sum_{j=1}^{N} (1-s_j) = Ae^{-t/\tau} \; ,$$

138

and another has been defined in Section 1 using the cosine function Γ. We compute the expected value at each time step and at the end of the run we fit a straight line to its logarithm by least squares to obtain the confinement time τ. For low collisionality a significant number of particles are lost, so in that case we consider the probability of a particle remaining in the plasma, too. The estimate using the expected value Γ defined in Section 1 gives the best measure of the confinement time for electrons because they can only be followed over a relatively short time interval. That all three expected values give comparable results is established by the relatively long calculation of escape times displayed in Fig. 32.

In this model of transport an electric potential Φ is included as described in Section 1. The electric potential and its first derivatives are evaluated in Subroutine ELPOT from Fourier coefficients P_{mn} which are defined by the parameters E0, E1, E2, and E3 in the input data file. The corresponding coefficients C_{mn} of the charge separation may be estimated by subtracting the Fourier coefficients F_{mn} of the distribution function output by the code for an ion run from those for an electron run. Since the Jacobian matrix relating C_{mn} to P_{mn} appears to be diagonally dominant in practice, a few runs can be used to find approximate roots P_{mn} of the quasineutrality equations $C_{mn} = 0$ (cf. Table 4).

The flow chart of the code is as follows. Two tapes from the equilibrium code are saved for a fine mesh run. Then a data file is used to prescribe numerical parameters and to initialize all variables in a deterministic way suggested by theory and practice. The number of particles followed is usually either 256 or 128. The code is vectorized with respect to this index. For electron runs the collision frequency $\bar{\nu}$ is divided in the code by the square root of the ratio of the ion mass to the electron mass. The input parameter TEND specifying the total time the orbits are followed is normally set at TEND = 1 for ions and

TEND = 2 for electrons. The value of SEED, which is used to initialize the random number generator RANF on the Cray, should be changed for each run to assure randomness. We have made an extensive study of accuracy parameters such as ACC, DELT, MF and NF to assure that there will be no significant error in final results. Convergence is monitored by the energy conservation parameter ENERCON. The two principal input parameters of the code are the dimensionless collision frequency FREQ and the dimensionless gyroradius RADL. A negative value of RADL is inserted for electron runs as an indicator for the code to perform necessary adjustments in the equations and scalings.

The input file DATA and the two equilibrium files Tape 2 and Tape 7 are named in the link card. Output appears on the file RUN, and Tapes 3 and 4 are used for storing results from the computation. The output file contains the input data file, data that identifies the equilibrium run from which Tapes 2 and 7 were taken, the Fourier coefficients of $1/B^2$, and the number of terms retained. This output is available before the Monte Carlo calculation is begun. After the orbits have been followed for half the length of the run, the Fourier coefficients of the distribution function are computed and printed. The difference of these coefficients for ion and electron runs serves to estimate the charge separation.

The final temperature, the number of lost particles, the collision time and the mean free path per field period are all printed. Confinement times are given using each of the three functionals discussed above, and at the end of the run two plots of the exponential decay of corresponding expected values are displayed. Examination of these two graphs helps to determine if the run is long enough in time and if enough orbits have been followed. A page of histograms follows giving the distributions of s and η. The code has been written so that if the sample of orbits is inadequate additional orbits can be calculated and included in the statistical estimate of the confinement

140

time. This is accomplished by setting NSTU to a value less than zero and reading in as Tape 4 the results of the previous run, which have been stored on Tape 3. At the end of the run these tapes are combined and stored on Tape 3 for future use. If a run is not long enough in time it can be extended as often as desired by setting NSTU > 0 again to save Tape 3 from the previous run and read it in as Tape 4. When runs are extended it is important that sufficient storage space be set aside by making the dimension NSTOR large enough in Subroutine TPLOT.

The collision frequency for electrons prescribed in the code should be the same as that for ions because it is automatically rescaled by a factor of 64 approximating the square root of the ratio of the ion and electron masses. When we make pairs of runs to compare the ions with the electrons, the specifications for both runs are the same except for the gyroradius. An electron run is indicated by a negative gyroradius whose absolute value is appropriate for electrons.

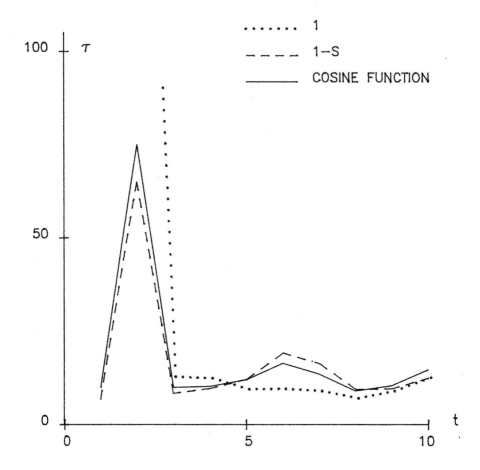

Fig. 32. Proof that three different expected values lead to equivalent estimates of the confinement time for electrons when the Monte Carlo calculation is performed over a long enough interval of time. The electron confinement time τ obtained from exponential decay of expected values of 1, 1-s, and the cosine function Γ are plotted in their dependence on the length of the run t.

142

3. Glossary of input parameters

CARDS 1,3,...,9   FORTRAN names of the parameters. Each parameter occupies 8 columns.

CARD 2

NS   The number of initial values for s; $s = 1-x^{1/2}$ with x evenly distributed over the interval $0 < x < 1$. FORMAT I8.

NPS1   The number of initial values for ψ, which are evenly distributed. FORMAT I8.

NPHI   The number of initial values for ϕ, which are evenly distributed. FORMAT I8.

NMAG   The number of initial values for the magnetic moment, which is input through the parameter $\eta = v_\parallel/v$. FORMAT I8.

NEK   The number of initial values for the kinetic energy. FORMAT I8.

NTE1,NTE2   Parameters in the background temperature profile
TE1 $T0*(1.0-TE1*SL2**NTE1)**NTE2$. FORMAT 2I8, F8.4.

CARD 4

FREQ   The collision frequency in units of the ion cyclotron frequency multiplied by 0.6E-06. Thus FREQ = 1 corresponds to reactor specifications. FORMAT F8.4.

FREQE   The collision frequency for energy scattering, in the same units as FREQ. Suggested value FREQE = FREQ. FORMAT F8.4.

DELT   The time interval for the collision operator multiplied by the collision frequency. The dimensionless time used in the code is measured in units of 10.**5 / ion cyclotron frequency. When B = 1 tesla the confinement time for protons comes out approximately in milliseconds. Suggested value DELT = 0.0025, but bigger values may be more economical for large FREQ. FORMAT F8.4.

TEND   The time of the run is proportional to TEND divided by SQRT(100*RADL*FREQ). FORMAT F8.4.

SEED   The initial value for the pseudorandom number generator. FORMAT F8.4.

SIZEL   A tolerance used to determine where the Fourier series for 1/(B*B) is truncated. FORMAT F8.4.

NPOL   The maximum exponent in the polynomial interpolation for 1/(B*B) as a function of s. Suggested value 2. FORMAT I8.

NCOL	The number of collisions during one interval of the ordinary differential equation solver. FORMAT I8.
CARD 6	
RADL	The gyroradius in units of the plasma radius. RADL should be negative for electrons. FORMAT F8.4.
E0,E1, E2,E3	Coefficients in the Fourier representation for the electric potential. The coding for the electric potential and its first derivatives can be modified in Subroutine ELPOT. FORMAT 4F8.4.
ACC	The exponent in the accuracy estimate for the ordinary differential equation solver. Suggested value 6.0. FORMAT F8.4.
MF	The maximum index of ψ terms in the Fourier series 1/(B*B). Suggested value 4. FORMAT I8.
NF	The maximum index of ϕ terms in the Fourier series for 1/(B*B). Suggested value 3. FORMAT I8.
CARD 8	
IC	A counter used to monitor printout. FORMAT I8.
NPRT	An indicator used to monitor printout. NRPT < 0 eliminates extra output. FORMAT I8.
TLIM	The estimated total CPU time for a run. FORMAT F8.4.
NRUN	The run number. FORMAT 6A8.
NSTU	An indicator for the type of run. NSTU = 0 for an isolated run, but NSTU > 0 for a run continued in time. Tape 3 is saved from the previous run, and it is input as Tape 4 for the continuation run. NSTU < 0 for the addition of orbits. A new set of orbits is calculated and combined with previous orbits stored in Tape 4. All the data is then stored in Tape 3 for future use. FORMAT I8.
NOFC	The number of Fourier coefficients of the distribution function. FORMAT I8.
TITLE	An identifying label for the runs. FORMAT 8A8.
CARDS 10,11,...	
M,N,K	The indices of the NOFC Fourier coefficients of the distribution function. Each Fourier coefficient is accounted for on a separate card, and N has to be renormalized when IROT = 1. FORMAT 3I8.

4. References

1. Y. Abe, "Three-dimensional MHD equilibrium and stability analysis code (BETA code)," Technical Report KAKEN-84-005, Institute of Plasma Physics, Nagoya University, 1984.

2. G. Bateman, MHD Instabilities, M.I.T. Press, Cambridge, 1978.

3. F. Bauer, O. Betancourt and P. Garabedian, A Computational Method in Plasma Physics, Springer-Verlag, New York, 1978.

4. F. Bauer, O. Betancourt and P. Garabedian, Magnetohydrodynamic Equilibrium and Stability of Stellarators, Springer-Verlag, New York, 1984.

5. F. Bauer, O. Betancourt and P. Garabedian, "Monte Carlo calculation of transport for three-dimensional magnetohydrodynamic equilibria," Comm. Pure Appl. Math. 39 (1986), 595-621.

6. F. Bauer, O. Betancourt, P. Garabedian and K. C. Ng, "Monte Carlo estimation of the electric field in stellarators," Proc. Natl. Acad. Sci. USA 83 (1986), 7565-7567.

7. O. Betancourt and P. Garabedian, "Computer simulation of the toroidal equilibrium and stability of a plasma in three dimensions," Proc. Natl. Acad. Sci. USA 72 (1975), 926-927.

8. O. Betancourt and P. Garabedian, "Confinement and transport in stellarators," Phys. Fluids 28 (1985), 912-919.

9. O. Betancourt and G. McFadden, "Nonparametric solutions to the variational principle of ideal magnetohydrodynamics," Analysis, Geometry and Probability: Proc. of the First Chilean Symposium, ed. by R. Chuaqi, Marcel Dekker, New York, 1985, 159-171.

10. A. Boozer, "Magnetic field Hamiltonian," Report PPPL-2094R, Princeton Plasma Physics Laboratory, Princeton University, 1984.

11. A. Boozer, "Ohm's law for mean magnetic fields," J. Plasma Phys. 35 (1986), 133-139.

12. A. Boozer and G. Kuo-Petravic, "Monte Carlo evaluation of transport coefficients," Phys. Fluids 24 (1981), 851-859.

13. M. Brambilla and A. Lichtenberg, "Drift-surface-island formation and particle diffusion in toroidal plasma," Nucl. Fusion 13 (1973), 517-520.

14. R. Fowler, J. Rome and J. Lyon, "Monte Carlo studies of transport in stellarators," Phys. Fluids 28 (1985), 338-344.

15. H. Grad, "Toroidal confinement of a plasma," Phys. Fluids 10 (1967), 137-154.

16. H. Grad, "The guiding center plasma," Amer. Math. Soc. Proc. Symp. Appl. Math.18 (1967), 162-248.

17. T. Hender, B. Carreras, L. Garcia, J. Rome and V. Lynch, "The calculation of stellarator equilibria in vacuum flux surface coordinates," J. Comput. Phys. 60 (1985), 76-96.

18. F. Herrnegger, "Numerical studies of magnetohydrostatic finite-beta stellarator equilibria," Zeit. Naturforsch. 37a (1982), 879-891.

19. S. Hirshman and J. Hogan, "ORMEC: A three dimensional MHD spectral inverse equilibrium code," ORNL Report ITM-9547, Oak Ridge National Laboratory, 1986.

20. J. Johnson, "MHD computations for stellarators," Comp. Phys. Reports 4 (1986), 37-69.

21. P. Lax, "Weak solutions of nonlinear hyperbolic equations and their numerical computation," Comm. Pure Appl. Math. 7 (1954), 159-193.

22. A. Lichtenberg and M. Lieberman, Regular and Stochastic Motion, Springer-Verlag, New York, 1983.

23. M. Marcal, "Magnetic and drift surfaces in toroidal plasma equilibria," Research and Development Report MF-98, Courant Institute, New York University, 1982.

24. K. Miyamoto, Plasma Physics for Nuclear Fusion, M.I.T. Press, Cambridge, 1976.

25. K. C. Ng, "Magnetic surfaces and neoclassical transport in stellarators," Ph.D. Thesis, New York University, 1987.

26. J. Nuehrenberg and R. Zille, "Stable stellarators with medium β and aspect ratio," Physics Letters 114A (1986), 129-132.

27. R. Potak, P. Politzer and L. Lidsky, "Ion thermal conductivity in a helical toroid," Phys. Rev. Lett. 45 (1980), 1328-1331.

28. F. Sano et al., "Particle and energy balance analysis of a currentless high beta plasma in Heliotron E," Nucl. Fusion 26 (1986), 473-481.

29. U. Schwenn, "Fourier versus difference methods in computing three-dimensional MHD equilibria," Comput. Phys. Commun. 31 (1984), 167-199.

30. E. Teller, Fusion, Academic Press, New York, 1981.

31. M. Wakatani, K. Ichiguchi, F. Bauer, O. Betancourt and P. Garabedian, "Stability calculations for the m = 1 / n = 1 mode in Heliotron configurations using the three-dimensional MHD equilibrium and stability (BETA) code," Nucl. Fusion 26 (1986), 1359-1370.

32. H. Wobig, "Numerical evaluation of neoclassical transport in stellarators at arbitrary collisionality," Zeit. Naturforsch. 37a (1982), 906-911.

V.   FORTRAN LISTING OF THE TRANSPORT CODE

```
C                    INDEX OF LIBRARY ROUTINES
C
C
C       RANSET  - ESTABLISH RANDOM NUMBER SEED               153
C       RANF    - OBTAIN RANDOM NUMBER              153,170,171
C       SECOND  - CUMULATIVE CPU TIME                   153,167
C       M01AJF  - SORT A VECTOR OF REAL NUMBERS; M01AJF,     159
C                 D02CHF, AND F04ATF ARE IN THE NAG LIBRARY
C       D02CHF  - INTEGRATE A SYSTEM OF FIRST ORDER         167
C                 ORDINARY DIFFERENTIAL EQUATIONS WITH
C                 INITIAL CONDITIONS USING A VARIABLE-
C                 ORDER VARIABLE-STEP ADAMS METHOD
C       F04ATF  - LINEAR EQUATION SOLVER                    176
C       KEEP80  - SAVE PLOT FILE FOR LATER USE              177
C       FR80ID  - MAKE A PLOT FILE                          177
C       MAP     - TRANSLATE AND SCALE PLOT                  177
C       FRAME   - ADVANCE FRAME                     178,180,181
C       GAXIS   - DRAW AND LABEL AXES                       186
C       SETLCH  - PLOT IN USER'S COORDINATES    177,178,180,186
C       CRTBCD  - WRITE LABELS ON AXES                      186
C       SETCRT  - SET INITIAL POSITION FOR PLOT             186
C       VECTOR  - DRAW A LINE                               186
C
C
C       THE DIMENSION STATEMENTS SHOULD BE COMPATIBLE WITH THOSE
C       IN TAPES 2 AND 7 FROM THE EQUILIBRIUM RUN OF CODE BETA.
C       CLICHE SPECIFICATIONS OF THE DIMENSION STATEMENTS ARE
C       LISTED BELOW. THE S, U, AND V DIMENSIONS ARE CHANGED IN THE
C       PARAMETER STATEMENT OF CLICHE NAMEA. THE PRECOMP UTILITY
C       PROCESSES PARAMETERS, CLICHES, AND ENDCLICHES. THE OUTPUT
C       OF PRECOMP CAN BE SUBMITTED TO THE FORTRAN COMPILER.
C
C
        CLICHE NAMEA
        PARAMETER(NID=13,NJD=24,NKD=24,NRUND=01,NIVD=01,NPART=256,
       1 IAD=10,IADD=1)
        ENDCLICHE
        CLICHE NAMEB
        USE NAMEA
        PARAMETER(ID=NID,JD=NJD+2,KD=NKD*NRUND+2,IV=NIVD,KP=5,NPT=NPART,
       1 NPT4=4*NPT)
        ENDCLICHE
        CLICHE NAME1
        USE NAMEB
        COMMON RO(ID,JD,KD),AL(ID,JD,KD),X(JD,KD),RA(KD),ZA(KD),
       1 R(JD,KD),Z(JD,KD),RU(JD,KD),ZU(JD,KD),RV(JD,KD),ZV(JD,KD)
        ENDCLICHE
        CLICHE NAME2
        USE NAMEB
        COMMON /INI/ PHIO(NPT),PSIO(NPT),SO(NPT),ETAO(NPT),AMAGO(NPT)
       1 ,NPAR,EKINO(NPT),TE1,NTE1,NTE2,TO
        ENDCLICHE
        CLICHE NAME3
        USE NAMEB
        COMMON /MC/ TJ(NPT),SJ(NPT),FREQ,RFREQ,SFREQ,SDELT,TSE,FTAU,
       1 T1,T2,NLOST,NCOL,NSTU,ICOL
        ENDCLICHE
        CLICHE NAME4
        USE NAMEB
        COMMON /POT/ PT(IV,JD,KD)
        ENDCLICHE
```

```
CLICHE NAME5
USE NAMEB
COMMON /INP/ Q(ID),QT(ID),AM(ID),PR(ID),QQ(ID),PC(ID),TC(ID)
1 ,NGEOM,SL1(ID),SL2(ID),MF,NF
ENDCLICHE
CLICHE NAME6
USE NAMEB
COMMON /CPL/ NI,NJ,NK,EP,ZLE,N1,N2,N3,N4,N5,NVAC,HS,HU,HV,
1 PI,IC,IO,IROT,FL(15),SNL2(ID),TLIM,ACC,NTER,KTER,NOR,TIMF
ENDCLICHE
CLICHE NAME7
USE NAMEB
COMMON /PHI/ ABL(11,7,ID),BBL(11,7,ID),CBL(11,7,ID),
1 DBL(11,7,ID),PHU1(ID,KD),PHV1(ID,KD),PHD(ID,KD),PHB2(ID,KD),
2 PPRIM(ID),BS2(ID),BS4(ID),BSAV(ID),BRIP(ID),ZTO(ID)
ENDCLICHE
CLICHE NAME8
USE NAMEB
COMMON /AUX/ U1(JD,KD),V1(JD,KD),B2(JD,KD),D(JD,KD),PHI(JD,KD),
1 PSI(JD,KD),PGL(ID,KD),PV3(ID,KD),PHPC(JD),PHTC(KD),BB(11,7,4),
2 CL(4),RL(11,7,4),COSPSI(11),SINPSI(11),COSPHI(7),SINPHI(7)
ENDCLICHE
CLICHE NAME9
USE NAMEB
COMMON /POL/ AB2(11,7,KP),BB2(11,7,KP),CB2(11,7,KP),DB2(11,7,KP),
1 TCC(KP),PCC(KP),QC(KP),QTC(KP),ZTOC(KP),PSC(KP),FLC(KP),NP,
2 TCI(ID),PCI(ID),QI(ID),QTI(ID),ZTOI(ID),FPI(ID),FACPI(ID),
3 PAS1(ID),PAS2(ID),PAS3(ID),PAS4(ID),PAS5(ID),PAS6(ID),
4 PAS7(ID),PAS8(ID),ASIG(11,7),BSIG(11,7),CSIG(11,7),DSIG(11,7)
5 ,ABE(ID),BBE(ID),CBE(ID),DBE(ID),RADL,EC,DELT,TEND,E0,XE0,E0C
6 ,SC1(ID),SC2(ID),CC1(ID),CC2(ID),SC1I(ID),SC2I(ID)
7 ,BMAXC(KP),BMINC(KP),BMAXI(ID),BMINI(ID),PI2,NPRT,IEL,
8 B2A(50,KP),B2B(50,KP),B2C(50,KP),B2D(50,KP),PCO,PRAD,E1,E2,E3
ENDCLICHE
CLICHE NAME10
USE NAMEB
COMMON /CHOICE/ ANOB(11,7),IB2MX,B2MAX,SB2MX,IB2MN,B2MIN,SB2MN,
1 BNOB(11,7),CNOB(11,7),DNOB(11,7),MAB2(50),MBB2(50),MCB2(50),
2 MDB2(50),NAB2(50),NBB2(50),NCB2(50),NDB2(50),SAB2(50),SBB2(50),
3 SCB2(50),SDB2(50),NUMA,NUMB,NUMC,NUMD,SIZEL,
4 MA2(50),MB2(50),MC2(50),MD2(50),NA2(50),NB2(50),NC2(50),ND2(50)
ENDCLICHE
CLICHE NAME11
USE NAMEB
COMMON /SOL/ B(NPT),BS(NPT),BPH(NPT),BPS(NPT),
1 ZET(NPT),ALAM(NPT),PSI(NPT),PHI(NPT),PS(NPT),ETA(NPT),AMAG(NPT),
2 ENER(NPT),ETAMA(NPT),ETAMI(NPT),PES1(NPT),PES2(NPT),PES3(NPT)
3 ,WORK(NPT4,18),EKIN(NPT),EKMAX(NPT),EKMIN(NPT),PES4(NPT),
4 PES5(NPT),PES6(NPT),POT(NPT),POTS(NPT),POTPH(NPT),POTPS(NPT)
ENDCLICHE
CLICHE NAME12
USE NAMEB
COMMON /EVAL/ FAV,GAV,ETAV,ETDV,PAV,SAV,SDV,DENER,NLEFT,FACS,TEAV,
1 TEMAX,TEMIN
ENDCLICHE
CLICHE NAME13
USE NAMEB
COMMON /PAS/ QX(NPT),QTX(NPT),PCX(NPT),TCX(NPT),ZTOX(NPT),
1 PSX(NPT),C1X(NPT),C2X(NPT),XT(KP,NPT),B2(NPT),B2S(NPT),B2PS(NPT),
2 S(NPT),S1(NPT),PSIT(NPT),PHIT(NPT),FACZ(NPT),FACPX(NPT),
3 AMN(NPT),AMNS(NPT),Y1(NPT),Y2(NPT),Y3(NPT),Y4(NPT),F1(NPT),
```

150

```
     4 F2(NPT),XX(NPT),XA(KP,NPT),FACX(NPT),CPS(8,NPT),SPS(8,NPT),
     5 CPH(4,NPT),SPH(4,NPT),B2PH(NPT),SFAC(NPT)
       ENDCLICHE
       CLICHE NAME14
       USE NAMEB
       DIMENSION Y(NPT4),F(NPT4)
       ENDCLICHE
       CLICHE NAME15
       USE NAMEB
       COMMON /PLOT/ PL(7000,10),IN(5)
       ENDCLICHE
       CLICHE NAME16
       USE NAMEB
       DIMENSION /ADD/ PL1(IADD,IAD),TP2(IADD),P1(IADD),P2(IADD),
     1 P3(IADD),PL2(IADD),TP1(IADD),FL1(IADD)
       ENDCLICHE
       CLICHE NAME17
       USE NAMEB
       COMMON /CONT/ YC(NPT4)
       ENDCLICHE
       CLICHE NAME18
       COMMON /FC/ NOFC,MO(10),NO(10),KO(10),FC(10),KOUNT,TEAVF
       ENDCLICHE
C
       PROGRAM BETAMOC (INPUT=65,OUTPUT=514,TAPE3=514,TAPE4=514,TAPE2=65
     1 ,TAPE1=514,TAPE25,TAPE7)
C      THIS MAIN ROUTINE CALLS OTHER SUBROUTINES
C      AND CONTROLS INPUT-OUTPUT
       DIMENSION FACP(101),TLAM(101)
       USE NAME1
       USE NAME2
       USE NAME3
       USE NAME4
       USE NAME5
       USE NAME6
       USE NAME7
       USE NAME9
       USE NAME10
       USE NAME15
       USE NAME17
       USE NAME18
       DIMENSION TITLE(4)
       CALL LINK ("UNIT25=(DATA,OPEN),UNIT6=(RUN,CREATE,TEXT),
     1 UNIT002=(TAPE2,OPEN,      ),UNIT003=(TAPE3,CREATE,     ),
     2 UNIT007=(TAPE7,OPEN,      ),UNIT004=(TAPE4,CREATE,     ),
     3 READ25,PRINT6//")
       READ (25,11)
       READ (25,20) NS,NPSI,NPHI,NMAG,NEKIN,NTE1,NTE2,TE1
       READ (25,11)
       READ (25,14) FREQ,FREQE,DELT,TEND,SEED,SIZEL,NP,NCOL
       READ (25,11)
       READ (25,30) RADL,E0,E1,E2,E3,ACC,NFU,NFV
       READ (25,11)
       READ (25,40) IC,NPRT,TLIM,NRUN,NSTU,NOFC,TITLE
       READ (25,11)
       DO 1 J=1,NOFC
     1 READ (25,50) MO(J),NO(J),KO(J)
       EC=0.5*RADL*RADL
       EOC=E0*EC
       PRINT 16
       PRINT 21,NS,NPSI,NPHI,NMAG,NEKIN,NTE1,NTE2,TE1
```

```
      PRINT 15,FREQ,FREQE,DELT,TEND,SEED,SIZEL,NP,NCOL
      IEL=1
      IF(RADL.LE.0.0) IEL=-1
      PRINT 22,RADL,E0,E1,E2,E3,ACC,NFU,NFV
      RADL=ABS(RADL)
      PRINT 23,IC,NPRT,TLIM,NRUN,NSTU,NOFC,TITLE
      PRINT 24
      DO 2 J=1,NOFC
    2 PRINT 26,MO(J),NO(J),KO(J)
      DO 3 J=1,NOFC
    3 FC(J)=0.0
      RTMASS=64.
      IF(IEL.LT.0) FREQ=FREQ/RTMASS
      IF(IEL.LT.0) FREQE=FREQE/RTMASS
      KOUNT=0
      TEAVF=0.0
      IF(NFU.GT.2*NP) NFU=2*NP
      NP=NP+1
      RFREQ=0.6E-06
      SFREQ=FREQ*RFREQ
      EFREQ=FREQE*RFREQ
      SDELT=DELT/AMAX1(SFREQ,EFREQ)
      TSE=TEND*SQRT(FREQ)/(10.*SFREQ*SQRT(RADL))
      FTAU=SDELT*SFREQ
      FTAUE=SDELT*EFREQ
      SDELT=SDELT*NCOL
      B2MAX=0.
      B2MIN=1.
C     READ EQUILIBRIUM RESULTS
      REWIND 7
      READ (7) NVAC,NI,NJ,NK,NUMB,IROT
      N1=NJ+1
      N2=NJ+2
      N3=NI-1
      N4=NK+1
      N5=NK+2
      READ (7) HS,HU,HV,EP,QLZ,RBOU,ZLE,PI
      READ (7) ((R(J,K),J=1,N2),K=1,N5),((Z(J,K),J=1,N2),K=1,N5)
      READ (7) ((RU(J,K),J=1,N2),K=1,N5),((ZU(J,K),J=1,N2),K=1,N5)
      READ (7) ((RV(J,K),J=1,N2),K=1,N5),((ZV(J,K),J=1,N2),K=1,N5)
      READ (7) (RA(K),K=1,N5),(ZA(K),K=1,N5)
      READ (7) (((RO(I,J,K),K=1,N5),J=1,N2),I=1,NI)
      READ (7) (((AL(I,J,K),K=1,N5),J=1,N2),I=1,NI)
      READ (7) (SL1(I),I=1,NI),(QT(I),I=1,NI),(Q(I),I=1,NI)
      READ (7) (SL2(I),I=1,NI),(PC(I),I=1,NI),(TC(I),I=1,NI)
      IF (NVAC.LT.0) GO TO 4
      READ (7) NIV,HR,C1,C2
      READ (7) ((X(J,K),K=1,N5),J=1,N2)
      READ (7) (((PT(I,J,K),K=1,N5),J=1,N2),I=1,NIV)
    4 CONTINUE
      READ (7) (SNL2(I),I=1,NI),MF,NF
      READ (7) (PR(I),I=2,N3),(PPRIM(I),I=2,N3)
      READ (7) (BRIP(I),I=1,NI),(QQ(I),I=1,NI)
      MF=MF-1
      NF=NF-1
      PRINT 200
      PRINT 201,EP,RBOU,QLZ,NUMB
      PRINT 202,NI,NJ,NK,NIV,NVAC
      PRINT 203,MF,NF,IROT,C1,C2
C     DEFINE CONSTANTS
      PI=3.1415926535898
```

```
      PI2=2.0*PI
      MF=NFU+1
      NF=NFV+1
      IO=50*IC
      DO 5 I=1,NI
      X1=-(PC(I)*QT(I)+TC(I)*Q(I))
      TLAM(I)=1.0/X1
    5 CONTINUE
      N3=NI-1
      DO 6 I=2,N3
      X1=(PC(I+1)-PC(I-1))/(SL2(I+1)-SL2(I-1))
      X2=(TC(I+1)-TC(I-1))/(SL2(I+1)-SL2(I-1))
      FACP(I)=TLAM(I)*(TC(I)*X1+PC(I)*X2)
    6 CONTINUE
      ISEED=ABS(SEED)
      CALL RANSET(ISEED)
      ICOL=0
      IF(NSTU.LE.0) GO TO 10
      REWIND 4
      DO 7 I=1,20000
      READ(4) (PL(I,J),J=1,10)
      IF(PL(I,1).LT.0.0) GO TO 8
    7 CONTINUE
    8 READ (4) X1,X2,TSE1,NM1,NM2,ICOL,NM4,NM5,NM8
      TSE=TSE+TSE1
      DO 9 I=1,ICOL
      X1=RANF(1)
      X2=RANF(1)
    9 CONTINUE
   10 CONTINUE
      CALL FPHI(PPRIM,FACP)
C     FOLLOWING TWO CARDS RESTORED IF E3 IS USED FOR LOOP VOLTAGE
C     PCO=-SIGN(1.0,TC(NI))*SFREQ*ZLE*RADL*E3/(PI2*PRAD)
C     IF(IEL.LT.0) PCO=PCO/43.0
      CALL SECOND(TIM2)
      CALL ORBIT(NS,NPHI,NPSI,NMAG,NEKIN,FTAUE)
      CALL SECOND(TIM3)
      PRINT 205
      TIMF=TIM3-TIM2
      CALL FPRINT
      CALL TPLOT(YC)
      IF(NPRT.LT.0) STOP
      PRINT 208,IB2MX,B2MAX,SB2MX
      PRINT 209,IB2MN,B2MIN,SB2MN
      STOP
C
   11 FORMAT(11A8)
   14 FORMAT(6F8.4,2I8)
   15 FORMAT(//,9X,4HFREQ,3X,5HFREQE,4X,4HDELT,4X,4HTEND,4X,4HSEED,3X
     1 ,5HSIZEL,4X,4HNPOL,4X,4HNCOL,/ 5X,4F8.4,F8.2,F8.4,2I8)
   16 FORMAT(///36X,5HINPUT,/)
   20 FORMAT(7I8,1F8.4)
   21 FORMAT(//,11X,2HNS,4X,4HNPSI,4X,4HNPHI,4X,4HNMAG,5X,3HNEK,4X,
     1 4HNTE1,4X,4HNTE2,5X,3HTE1,/5X,7I8,F8.4)
   22 FORMAT(//,9X,4HRADL,6X,2HE0,6X,2HE1,6X,2HE2,6X,2HE3,5X,
     1 3HACC,6X,"MF",6X,"NF"/5X,F8.5,4F8.4,F8.4,2I8)
   23 FORMAT(/,11X,2HIC,4X,4HNPRT,4X,4HTLIM,4X,4HNRUN,4X,4HNSTU,
     1 4X,4HNOFC,11X,5HTITLE/5X,2I8,F8.1,3I8,4A8)
   24 FORMAT(//10X,"FOURIER COEFFICIENTS OF DISTRIBUTION FUNCTION",//
     1 ,12X,"M",7X,"N",7X,"K",/)
   26 FORMAT(5X,3I8)
```

```fortran
   30 FORMAT(F8.5,5F8.4,2I8)
   40 FORMAT(2I8,F8.2,I8,I8,I8,4A8)
   50 FORMAT(3I8)
  200 FORMAT(/////18X,"DATA USED FROM EQUILIBRIUM RUN",/)
  201 FORMAT(11X,2HEP,4X,4HRBOU,5X,3HQLZ,5X,3HRUN/6X,3(F7.4,1X),2X,I5//)
  202 FORMAT(11X,2HNI,6X,2HNJ,6X,2HNK,5X,3HNIV,4X,4HNVAC/5X,5(3X,I5),//)
  203 FORMAT(11X,2HMF,6X,2HNF,4X,4HIROT,6X,2HC1,6X,2HC2/5X,3(3X,I5),2(1X
     1 ,F7.4)//)
  204 FORMAT(7H NLEFT=I6)
  205 FORMAT(//////,35X,"OUTPUT",//)
  208 FORMAT(//,7H IB2MX=I5,7H B2MAX=E16.8,7H SB2MX=E16.8/)
  209 FORMAT(7H IB2MN=I5,7H B2MIN=E16.8,7H SB2MN=E16.8/)
      END


      SUBROUTINE FPHI(FP,FACP)
C     COMPUTES FOURIER COEFFICIENTS OF FIELD IN FLUX COORDINATES
      USE NAME1
      USE NAME5
      USE NAME6
      USE NAME7
      USE NAME8
      USE NAME9
      USE NAME10
      DIMENSION FP(101),ZPE(50)
      DIMENSION FACP(101),WKS1(10),WKS2(10),BMAX(101),BMIN(101)
      MFT=MF
      NFT=NF
      DUV=HU*HV
      DO 281 I=2,N3
      X1=QT(I)*PC(I)+Q(I)*TC(I)
      FAC=-4.0/X1
      FAC1=FAC*DUV
      FACZ=FP(I)*X1/(2.0*PI*QT(I))
      BS4(I)=0.0
      BSAV(I)=0.0
      TOT=0.0
      REWIND 2
      SAV=0.0
      DO 30 J=2,N1
      READ(2) ((PHV1(I9,K),I9=2,N3),K=2,N4),((PHU1(I9,K),I9=2,N3),K=2,
     1 N4),((PHD(I9,K),I9=2,N3),K=2,N4),((PHB2(I9,K),I9=2,N3),K=2,N4),
     1 ((PGL(I9,K),I9=2,N3),K=2,N4),((PV3(I9,K),I9=2,N3),K=2,N4)
      DO 30 K=2,N4
      U1(J,K)=PHU1(I,K)
      V1(J,K)=PHV1(I,K)
      D(J,K)=PHD(I,K)
      SAV=SAV+HU*HV*PHD(I,K)
      B2(J,K)=PHB2(I,K)
      BS4(I)=BS4(I)+0.25*FAC*HU*HV*D(J,K)/B2(J,K)
      BSAV(I)=BSAV(I)+HU*HV*B2(J,K)*B2(J,K)
      TOT=TOT+HU*HV*B2(J,K)
   30 CONTINUE
      READ (2) (ZTO(II),II=2,N3),(BMAX(II),II=2,N3),(BMIN(II),II=2,N3)
      BSAV(I)=SQRT(BSAV(I)/TOT)
      N33=N3-1
      II=(NI+1)/2
C     COMPUTE SCALAR POTENTIAL PHI
      PHI(1,1)=0.0
      DO 40 K=2,N4
   40 PHI(1,K)=PHI(1,K-1)-HV*V1(N1,K)
```

```
      DO 60 J=2,N1
      U1(J,1)=U1(J,N4)
      DO 50 K=1,N4
   50 PHI(J,K)=PHI(J-1,K)-HU*U1(J,K)
   60 PHPC(J)=PHI(J,N4)-PHI(J,1)
      DO 70 K=2,N4
   70 PHTC(K)=PHI(N1,K)-PHI(1,K)
      SUMPC=0.0
      SUMTC=0.0
      DO 80 J=2,N1
   80 SUMPC=SUMPC+HU*PHPC(J)
      DO 90 K=2,N4
   90 SUMTC=SUMTC+HV*PHTC(K)
      PC(I)=SUMPC
      TC(I)=SUMTC
C     NORMALIZE PERIODS OF POTENTIAL PHI AND FLUX PSI
      DO 100 J=2,N1
      DO 100 K=2,N4
      X1=PHI(J,K)
      X2=0.25*(AL(I,J,K)+AL(I,J+1,K)+AL(I,J,K+1)+AL(I,J+1,K+1))
      X3=PC(I)+Q(I)*TC(I)/QT(I)
      PHI(J,K)=2.0*PI*(X1+TC(I)*X2/QT(I))/X3
  100 PSI(J,K)=-2.0*PI*(X2-Q(I)*X1/PC(I))*PC(I)/(QT(I)*X3)
      SUM1=0.0
      SUM2=0.0
      DO 110 J=2,N1
  110 SUM1=SUM1+HU*PHI(J,2)
      DO 120 K=2,N4
  120 SUM2=SUM2+HV*PSI(2,K)
      SC1(I)=SUM2
      SC2(I)=SUM1
      DO 130 J=2,N1
      DO 130 K=2,N4
      PHI(J,K)=PHI(J,K)-SUM1
  130 PSI(J,K)=PSI(J,K)-SUM2
      DO 140 J=2,N1
      DO 140 K=2,N4
  140 V1(J,K)=SQRT(B2(J,K))
      DO 160 M=1,MFT
      DO 160 N=1,NFT
      DO 160 L=1,4
      BB(M,N,L)=0.0
  160 CONTINUE
C     COMPUTE FOURIER COEFFICIENTS OF 1/(B*B) AND PARALLEL CURRENT
      DO 183 J=2,N1
      DO 183 K=2,N4
      DO 180 M=1,MFT
      COSPSI(M)=COS((M-1)*PSI(J,K))
  180 SINPSI(M)=SIN((M-1)*PSI(J,K))
      DO 181 N=1,NFT
      COSPHI(N)=COS((N-1)*PHI(J,K))
  181 SINPHI(N)=SIN((N-1)*PHI(J,K))
      X6=FAC1*D(J,K)
      DO 183 M=1,MFT
      DO 183 N=1,NFT
      CL(1)=COSPSI(M)*COSPHI(N)
      CL(2)=COSPSI(M)*SINPHI(N)
      CL(3)=SINPSI(M)*COSPHI(N)
      CL(4)=SINPSI(M)*SINPHI(N)
      DO 182 L=1,4
      FAC2=X6*CL(L)
```

```
         BB(M,N,L)=BB(M,N,L)+FAC2
182 CONTINUE
183 CONTINUE
         DO 191 L=1,4
191 RL(1,1,L)=0.0
         DO 200 M=1,MFT
         DO 200 L=1,4
         BB(M,1,L)=BB(M,1,L)/2.0
200 CONTINUE
         DO 210 N=1,NFT
         DO 210 L=1,4
         BB(1,N,L)=BB(1,N,L)/2.0
210 CONTINUE
         BS2(I)=0.0
         DO 240 L=1,4
         BS2(I)=BS2(I)+BB(1,1,L)*BB(1,1,L)
         DO 220 M=2,MFT
220 BS2(I)=BS2(I)+0.5*BB(M,1,L)*BB(M,1,L)
         DO 230 N=2,NFT
230 BS2(I)=BS2(I)+0.5*BB(1,N,L)*BB(1,N,L)
         DO 240 M=2,MFT
         DO 240 N=2,NFT
240 BS2(I)=BS2(I)+0.25*BB(M,N,L)*BB(M,N,L)
         AMUL=0.000001
C     COMPUTE FOURIER COEFFICIENTS OF PARALLEL CURRENT FROM
C     FOURIER COEFFICIENTS OF 1/(B*B)
         DO 260 M=1,MFT
         DO 260 N=1,NFT
         X2=(N-1.)-(M-1.)*Q(I)/QT(I)
         IF(ABS(X2).LT.AMUL) X2=SIGN(AMUL,X2)
         X4=(N-1.0)+(M-1.0)*Q(I)/QT(I)
         IF(ABS(X4).LT.AMUL) X4=SIGN(AMUL,X4)
         IF(M.EQ.1.AND.N.EQ.1) GO TO 250
         Y1=0.5*(BB(M,N,1)+BB(M,N,4))
         Y2=0.5*(BB(M,N,1)-BB(M,N,4))
         Y3=0.5*(BB(M,N,3)+BB(M,N,2))
         Y4=0.5*(BB(M,N,3)-BB(M,N,2))
         RL(M,N,1)=FACZ*(Y4/X2-Y3/X4)
         RL(M,N,4)=FACZ*(Y4/X2+Y3/X4)
         RL(M,N,3)=FACZ*(Y2/X4-Y1/X2)
         RL(M,N,2)=FACZ*(Y2/X4+Y1/X2)
250 CONTINUE
         ABL(M,N,I)=BB(M,N,1)
         BBL(M,N,I)=BB(M,N,2)
         CBL(M,N,I)=BB(M,N,3)
         DBL(M,N,I)=BB(M,N,4)
260 CONTINUE
C     COMPUTE PARALLEL CURRENT FROM ITS FOURIER SERIES
         ZPE(I)=0.0
         DO 280 J=2,N1
         DO 280 K=2,N4
         U1(J,K)=0.0
         X1=PSI(J,K)+SC1(I)
         X2=PHI(J,K)+SC2(I)
         DO 261 M=1,MFT
         COSPSI(M)=COS((M-1)*PSI(J,K))
261 SINPSI(M)=SIN((M-1)*PSI(J,K))
         DO 262 N=1,NFT
         COSPHI(N)=COS((N-1)*PHI(J,K))
262 SINPHI(N)=SIN((N-1)*PHI(J,K))
         DO 265 M=1,MFT
```

```
      DO 265 N=1,NFT
      CL(1)=COSPSI(M)*COSPHI(N)
      CL(2)=COSPSI(M)*SINPHI(N)
      CL(3)=SINPSI(M)*COSPHI(N)
      CL(4)=SINPSI(M)*SINPHI(N)
      DO 264 L=1,4
      U1(J,K)=U1(J,K)+CL(L)*RL(M,N,L)
  264 CONTINUE
  265 CONTINUE
      ZPE(I)=ZPE(I)+DUV*U1(J,K)
  280 CONTINUE
  281 CONTINUE
      DO 283 I=2,N3
  283 ZTO(I)=ZTO(I)-ZPE(I)
      B0=BNORM(3,N33,SL2,BSAV,SL1(3),SL1(N33))
      PRAD=0.0
      DO 284 J=2,N1
      DO 284 K=2,N4
      X1=R(J,K)-0.5*(RA(K)+RA(K+1))
      X2=Z(J,K)-0.5*(ZA(K)+ZA(K+1))
  284 PRAD=PRAD+DUV*SQRT(X1*X1+X2*X2)
      PRINT 312,B0,PRAD
C     SCALE FIELD AND CURRENT
      BD=B0*PRAD
      B02=B0*B0
      DO 285 I=2,N3
      ZTO(I)=ZTO(I)/BD
      FP(I)=FP(I)/B02
      Q(I)=Q(I)/(B0*PRAD*PRAD)
      QT(I)=QT(I)/(B0*PRAD*PRAD)
      PC(I)=PC(I)/BD
      TC(I)=TC(I)/BD
      FACP(I)=FACP(I)*PRAD
      DO 285 M=1,MFT
      DO 285 N=1,NFT
      ABL(M,N,I)=ABL(M,N,I)*B02
      BBL(M,N,I)=BBL(M,N,I)*B02
      CBL(M,N,I)=CBL(M,N,I)*B02
  285 DBL(M,N,I)=DBL(M,N,I)*B02
      CALL PINT(2,3,2,N3,1.0,SL2,TC,TCI,TCC,SIG1)
      CALL PINT(0,3,2,N3,1.0,SL2,PC,PCI,PCC ,SIG2)
      CALL PINT(0,3,2,N3,1.0,SL2,Q ,QI ,QC ,SIG3)
      CALL PINT(0,3,2,N3,1.0,SL2,QT ,QTI ,QTC ,SIG4)
      CALL PINT(0,3,2,N3,1.0,SL2,ZTO ,ZTOI ,ZTOC ,SIG5)
      CALL PINT(0,3,2,N3,1.0,SL2,FP ,FPI ,PSC ,SIG6)
      CALL PINT(0,3,2,N3,1.0,SL2,FACP ,FACPI ,FLC ,SIG7)
      CALL PINT(0,3,2,N3,1.0,SL2,SC1,SC1I,CC1,SIG8)
      CALL PINT(0,3,2,N3,1.0,SL2,SC2,SC2I,CC2,SIG9)
      CALL PINT(0,3,2,N3,1.0,SL2,BMAX,BMAXI,BMAXC,SIG10)
      CALL PINT(0,3,2,N3,1.0,SL2,BMIN,BMINI,BMINC,SIG11)
      IF(NPRT.LT.0) GO TO 287
      PRINT 320
      DO 286 I=2,N3
  286 PRINT 322,TC(I),TCI(I),PC(I),PCI(I),Q(I),QI(I),QT(I),QTI(I),
     1 ZTO(I),ZTOI(I),FP(I),FPI(I),FACP(I),FACPI(I),BMAX(I),BMAXI(I)
      PRINT 323,SIG1,SIG2,SIG3,SIG4,SIG5,SIG6,SIG7,SIG10
  287 CONTINUE
      DO 297 M=1,MFT
      ML=M-1
      NPO=NPOL(ML)
      DO 297 N=1,NFT
```

```
      DO 288 I=2,N3
      PAS1(I)=0.5*(ABL(M,N,I)+DBL(M,N,I))
      PAS2(I)=0.5*(ABL(M,N,I)-DBL(M,N,I))
      PAS3(I)=0.5*(CBL(M,N,I)+BBL(M,N,I))
      PAS4(I)=0.5*(CBL(M,N,I)-BBL(M,N,I))
  288 CONTINUE
      ANOB(M,N)=BNORM(2,N3,SL2,PAS1,SL1(2),SL1(N3))
      BNOB(M,N)=BNORM(2,N3,SL2,PAS2,SL1(2),SL1(N3))
      CNOB(M,N)=BNORM(2,N3,SL2,PAS3,SL1(2),SL1(N3))
      DNOB(M,N)=BNORM(2,N3,SL2,PAS4,SL1(2),SL1(N3))
      DO 289 K=1,NP
      PAS5(K)=0.0
      PAS6(K)=0.0
      PAS7(K)=0.0
  289 PAS8(K)=0.0
      CALL PINT(ML,NPO,2,N3,1.0,SL2,PAS1,ABE,PAS5,ASIG(M,N))
      CALL PINT(ML,NPO,2,N3,1.0,SL2,PAS2,BBE,PAS6,BSIG(M,N))
      CALL PINT(ML,NPO,2,N3,1.0,SL2,PAS3,CBE,PAS7,CSIG(M,N))
      CALL PINT(ML,NPO,2,N3,1.0,SL2,PAS4,DBE,PAS8,DSIG(M,N))
      DO 290 K=1,NPO
      AB2(M,N,K)=PAS5(K)
      BB2(M,N,K)=PAS6(K)
      CB2(M,N,K)=PAS7(K)
  290 DB2(M,N,K)=PAS8(K)
  297 CONTINUE
      CALL CHOICE
      RETURN
C
  305 FORMAT(3X,6F10.3)
  312 FORMAT(7X,"BO =",F6.3,23X,"AVERAGE PLASMA RADIUS =",F6.3,//)
  320 FORMAT(///,6X,"TC",6X,"TCI",5X,"PC",6X,"PCI",5X,"Q",
     1 7X,"QI",6X,"QT",6X,"QTI",5X,"ZTO",5X,"ZTOI",4X,"PP",
     2 6X,"PPI",5X,"FLC",5X,"FLCI",4X,"BMAX",3X,"BMAXI",//)
  322 FORMAT(3X,16F8.3)
  323 FORMAT(/,3X,"SIGMA=",2X,8(F8.4,8X))
      END


      SUBROUTINE CHOICE
C     OPTIMAL TRUNCATION OF FOURIER SERIES
      USE NAME5
      USE NAME9
      USE NAME10
      DIMENSION IR1(50),ASB2(50),BSB2(50),CSB2(50),DSB2(50),IRA(50)
     1 ,IRB(50),IRC(50),IRD(50),IMAB2(50),IMBB2(50),IMCB2(50),IMDB2(50),
     2 INAB2(50),INBB2(50),INCB2(50),INDB2(50)
      NJ=MF*NF
      DO 1 N=1,NF
      DO 1 M=1,MF
      J=M+(N-1)*MF
      BSB2(J)=BNOB(M,N)
      CSB2(J)=CNOB(M,N)
      DSB2(J)=DNOB(M,N)
      IRA(J)=J
      IRB(J)=J
      IRC(J)=J
      IRD(J)=J
      IMAB2(J)=M-1
      IMBB2(J)=M-1
      IMCB2(J)=M-1
      IMDB2(J)=M-1
```

```
      INAB2(J)=N-1
      INBB2(J)=N-1
      INCB2(J)=N-1
      INDB2(J)=N-1
    1 ASB2(J)=ANOB(M,N)
      IFAIL=0
      CALL M01AJF(ASB2,SAB2,IRA,IR1,NJ,50,IFAIL)
      CALL M01AJF(BSB2,SBB2,IRB,IR1,NJ,50,IFAIL)
      CALL M01AJF(CSB2,SCB2,IRC,IR1,NJ,50,IFAIL)
      CALL M01AJF(DSB2,SDB2,IRD,IR1,NJ,50,IFAIL)
      IF(IFAIL.EQ.0) GO TO 9
      PRINT 115,IFAIL
      STOP27
    9 CONTINUE
      NUMA=0
      NUMB=0
      NUMC=0
      NUMD=0
      DO 20 J=1,NJ
      JJ=IRA(NJ-J+1)
      MAB2(J)=IMAB2(JJ)
      NAB2(J)=INAB2(JJ)
      SAB2(J)=ASB2(NJ-J+1)
      JJ=IRB(NJ-J+1)
      MBB2(J)=IMBB2(JJ)
      NBB2(J)=INBB2(JJ)
      SBB2(J)=BSB2(NJ-J+1)
      JJ=IRC(NJ-J+1)
      MCB2(J)=IMCB2(JJ)
      NCB2(J)=INCB2(JJ)
      SCB2(J)=CSB2(NJ-J+1)
      JJ=IRD(NJ-J+1)
      MDB2(J)=IMDB2(JJ)
      NDB2(J)=INDB2(JJ)
      SDB2(J)=DSB2(NJ-J+1)
      IF(SAB2(J).LT.SIZEL) GO TO 15
      NUMA=J
   15 IF(SBB2(J).LT.SIZEL) GO TO 16
      NUMB=J
   16 IF(SCB2(J).LT.SIZEL) GO TO 17
      NUMC=J
   17 IF(SDB2(J).LT.SIZEL) GO TO 18
      NUMD=J
   18 CONTINUE
      DO 19 K=1,NP
      B2A(J,K)=AB2(MAB2(J)+1,NAB2(J)+1,K)
      B2B(J,K)=BB2(MBB2(J)+1,NBB2(J)+1,K)
      B2C(J,K)=CB2(MCB2(J)+1,NCB2(J)+1,K)
   19 B2D(J,K)=DB2(MDB2(J)+1,NDB2(J)+1,K)
   20 CONTINUE
      DO 21 J=1,NJ
      MA2(J)=MAB2(J)+1
      NA2(J)=NAB2(J)+1
      MB2(J)=MBB2(J)+1
      NB2(J)=NBB2(J)+1
      MC2(J)=MCB2(J)+1
      NC2(J)=NCB2(J)+1
      ND2(J)=NDB2(J)+1
   21 MD2(J)=MDB2(J)+1
      PRINT 28
      PRINT 31
```

```
      PRINT 29,NUMA,NUMB,NUMD,NUMC
      PRINT 30
      PRINT 114
      PRINT 100
      PRINT 101
      PRINT 110
      DO 22 J=1,NJ
   22 PRINT 112,J,MAB2(J),NAB2(J),SAB2(J),(B2A(J,K),K=1,NP)
      PRINT 103
      PRINT 110
      DO 23 J=1,NJ
   23 PRINT 112,J,MBB2(J),NBB2(J),SBB2(J),(B2B(J,K),K=1,NP)
      IF(NPRT.LT.0) GO TO 25
      PRINT 102
      PRINT 116
      DO 24 J=1,NJ
   24 PRINT 113,J,MCB2(J),NCB2(J),SCB2(J),(B2C(J,K),K=1,NP),MDB2(J),
     1 NDB2(J),SDB2(J),(B2D(J,K),K=1,NP)
   25 CONTINUE
      RETURN
C
   28 FORMAT(39X,"C(M-N)",2X,"C(M+N)",2X,"S(M+N)",2X,"S(M-N)")
   29 FORMAT(7X,"REPRESENTING MAGNETIC FIELD"3X,4I8)
   30 FORMAT(//////)
   31 FORMAT(7X,"NUMBER OF FOURIER TERMS")
  100 FORMAT(///24X,"FOURIER COEFFICIENTS OF 1/B*B",///)
  101 FORMAT(29X,"COS(M PSI - N PHI)",/)
  102 FORMAT(///,28X,"SIN(M PSI - N PHI)",30X,"SIN(M PSI + N PHI)",/)
  103 FORMAT(//29X,"COS(M PSI + N PHI)",/)
  110 FORMAT(/,7X,"J",4X,"M",4X,"N",8X,"NORM",9X,"1",6X,"S",3X,"S**2"/)
  112 FORMAT(3X,3I5,E12.3,3X,3F7.3)
  113 FORMAT(2X,3I5,E12.3,3X,3F7.3,2X,2I5,E12.3,3X,3F7.3)
  114 FORMAT(//)
  115 FORMAT(///,3X,"IFAIL=",I3)
  116 FORMAT(//,6X,"J",4X,"M",4X,"N",8X,"NORM",9X,"1",6X,"S",3X,"S**2
     1 ",3X,"M",4X,"N",8X,"NORM",9X,"1",6X,"S",3X,"S**2",/)
      END


      SUBROUTINE BVAL(Y)
C     EVALUATION OF THE MAGNETIC FIELD
      USE NAME5
      USE NAME6
      USE NAME9
      USE NAME10
      USE NAME11
      USE NAME12
      USE NAME13
      USE NAME14
      AMUL=0.0000001
      DO 101 I=1,NLEFT
      B2(I)=0.0
      B2S(I)=0.0
      B2PS(I)=0.0
      B2PH(I)=0.0
      ZET(I)=0.0
      ALAM(I)=0.0
      S(I)=Y(4*I-3)
      PSIT(I)=Y(4*I-2)
  101 PHIT(I)=Y(4*I-1)
      DO 103 I=1,NLEFT
```

160

```
      IF(S(I).GE.0.0) GO TO 102
      PRINT 280,S(I)
      STOP77
102   S1(I)=SQRT(S(I))
103   CONTINUE
      DO 104 I=1,NLEFT
104   XT(1,I)=1.0
      DO 205 K=2,3
      DO 105 I=1,NLEFT
105   XT(K,I)=XT(K-1,I)*S(I)
205   CONTINUE
      DO 206 I=1,NLEFT
      QX(I)=0.0
      QTX(I)=0.0
      PCX(I)=0.0
      TCX(I)=0.0
      ZTOX(I)=0.0
      FACPX(I)=0.0
      PSX(I)=0.0
      C1X(I)=0.0
206   C2X(I)=0.0
      DO 208 K=1,3
      DO 207 I=1,NLEFT
      C1X(I)=C1X(I)+XT(K,I)*CC1(K)
      C2X(I)=C2X(I)+XT(K,I)*CC2(K)
      TCX(I)=TCX(I)+XT(K,I)*TCC(K)*S(I)
      PCX(I)=PCX(I)+XT(K,I)*PCC(K)
      QX(I)=QX(I)+XT(K,I)*QC(K)
      QTX(I)=QTX(I)+XT(K,I)*QTC(K)
      ZTOX(I)=ZTOX(I)+XT(K,I)*ZTOC(K)
      FACPX(I)=FACPX(I)+XT(K,I)*FLC(K)
207   PSX(I)=PSX(I)+XT(K,I)*PSC(K)
208   CONTINUE
      DO 209 I=1,NLEFT
209   PES1(I)=QTX(I)*PCX(I)+QX(I)*TCX(I)
      DO 210 I=1,NLEFT
      FACX(I)=QX(I)/QTX(I)
      FACZ(I)=PSX(I)*PES1(I)/(PI2*QTX(I))
      PSI(I)=-((PSIT(I)+C1X(I))*QTX(I)-(PHIT(I)+C2X(I))*QX(I))/PI2
      PHI(I)=((PSIT(I)+C1X(I))*TCX(I)+(PHIT(I)+C2X(I))*PCX(I))/PI2
210   XT(1,I)=1.0
      DO 212 K=2,NP
      DO 211 I=1,NLEFT
211   XT(K,I)=XT(K-1,I)*S(I)
212   CONTINUE
      DO 214 M=1,MF
      DO 213 I=1,NLEFT
      CPS(M,I)=COS((M-1)*PSIT(I))
213   SPS(M,I)=SIN((M-1)*PSIT(I))
214   CONTINUE
      DO 216 N=1,NF
      DO 215 I=1,NLEFT
      CPH(N,I)=COS((N-1)*PHIT(I))
215   SPH(N,I)=SIN((N-1)*PHIT(I))
216   CONTINUE
      IF(NUMA.EQ.0) GO TO 230
      DO 229 J=1,NUMA
      MM=MAB2(J)
      NPO=NPOL(MM)
      NN=NAB2(J)
      MM1=MA2(J)
```

161

```
        NN1=NA2(J)
        DO 217 I=1,NLEFT
        AMN(I)=0.0
217     AMNS(I)=0.0
        DO 219 K=1,NPO
        DO 218 I=1,NLEFT
218     XA(K,I)=XT(K,I)*B2A(J,K)
219     CONTINUE
        DO 220 I=1,NLEFT
        Y1(I)=CPS(MM1,I)
        Y2(I)=SPS(MM1,I)
        Y3(I)=CPH(NN1,I)
220     Y4(I)=SPH(NN1,I)
        DO 221 I=1,NLEFT
        F1(I)=Y1(I)*Y3(I)+Y2(I)*Y4(I)
        F2(I)=Y2(I)*Y3(I)-Y1(I)*Y4(I)
        XX(I)=NN-MM*FACX(I)
221     SFAC(I)=S1(I)**MM
        DO 222 I=1,NLEFT
        IF(ABS(XX(I)).LT.AMUL)XX(I)=SIGN(AMUL,XX(I))
222     CONTINUE
        DO 224 K=1,NPO
        FK=K-1+0.5*MM
        DO 223 I=1,NLEFT
        AMN(I)=AMN(I)+XA(K,I)
223     AMNS(I)=AMNS(I)+XA(K,I)*FK
224     CONTINUE
        DO 225 I=1,NLEFT
        AMN(I)=AMN(I)*SFAC(I)
225     AMNS(I)=AMNS(I)*SFAC(I)/S(I)
        DO 226 I=1,NLEFT
        B2(I)=B2(I)+AMN(I)*F1(I)
        B2S(I)=B2S(I)+AMNS(I)*F1(I)
        B2PS(I)=B2PS(I)-AMN(I)*MM*F2(I)
226     B2PH(I)=B2PH(I)+AMN(I)*NN*F2(I)
        DO 227 I=1,NLEFT
        Y1(I)=AMN(I)*F1(I)*(MM*PCX(I)+NN*TCX(I))/(QTX(I)*XX(I))
227     Y2(I)=AMN(I)*F2(I)*FACZ(I)/XX(I)
        DO 228 I=1,NLEFT
        IF(MM.EQ.0.AND.NN.EQ.0) GO TO 228
        ALAM(I)=ALAM(I)-Y1(I)
        ZET(I)=ZET(I)-Y2(I)
228     CONTINUE
229     CONTINUE
230     IF(NUMB.EQ.0) GO TO 244
        DO 243 J=1,NUMB
        MM=MBB2(J)
        NPO=NPOL(MM)
        NN=NBB2(J)
        MM1=MB2(J)
        NN1=NB2(J)
        DO 231 I=1,NLEFT
        AMN(I)=0.0
231     AMNS(I)=0.0
        DO 233 K=1,NPO
        DO 232 I=1,NLEFT
232     XA(K,I)=XT(K,I)*B2B(J,K)
233     CONTINUE
        DO 234 I=1,NLEFT
        Y1(I)=CPS(MM1,I)
        Y2(I)=SPS(MM1,I)
```

```
          Y3(I)=CPH(NN1,I)
234       Y4(I)=SPH(NN1,I)
          DO 235 I=1,NLEFT
          F1(I)=Y1(I)*Y3(I)-Y2(I)*Y4(I)
          F2(I)=Y2(I)*Y3(I)+Y1(I)*Y4(I)
          XX(I)=NN+MM*FACX(I)
235       SFAC(I)=S1(I)**MM
          DO 236 I=1,NLEFT
          IF(ABS(XX(I)).LT.AMUL)XX(I)=SIGN(AMUL,XX(I))
236       CONTINUE
          DO 238 K=1,NPO
          FK=K-1+0.5*MM
          DO 237 I=1,NLEFT
          AMN(I)=AMN(I)+XA(K,I)
237       AMNS(I)=AMNS(I)+XA(K,I)*FK
238       CONTINUE
          DO 239 I=1,NLEFT
          AMN(I)=AMN(I)*SFAC(I)
239       AMNS(I)=AMNS(I)*SFAC(I)/S(I)
          DO 240 I=1,NLEFT
          B2(I)=B2(I)+AMN(I)*F1(I)
          B2S(I)=B2S(I)+AMNS(I)*F1(I)
          B2PS(I)=B2PS(I)-AMN(I)*MM*F2(I)
240       B2PH(I)=B2PH(I)-AMN(I)*NN*F2(I)
          DO 241 I=1,NLEFT
          Y1(I)=AMN(I)*F1(I)*(MM*PCX(I)-NN*TCX(I))/(QTX(I)*XX(I))
241       Y2(I)=AMN(I)*F2(I)*FACZ(I)/XX(I)
          DO 242 I=1,NLEFT
          IF(MM.EQ.0.AND.NN.EQ.0) GO TO 242
          ALAM(I)=ALAM(I)+Y1(I)
          ZET(I)=ZET(I)+Y2(I)
242       CONTINUE
243       CONTINUE
244       IF(NUMC.EQ.0) GO TO 258
          DO 257 J=1,NUMC
          MM=MCB2(J)
          NPO=NPOL(MM)
          NN=NCB2(J)
          MM1=MC2(J)
          NN1=NC2(J)
          DO 245 I=1,NLEFT
          AMN(I)=0.0
245       AMNS(I)=0.0
          DO 247 K=1,NPO
          DO 246 I=1,NLEFT
246       XA(K,I)=XT(K,I)*B2C(J,K)
247       CONTINUE
          DO 248 I=1,NLEFT
          Y1(I)=CPS(MM1,I)
          Y2(I)=SPS(MM1,I)
          Y3(I)=CPH(NN1,I)
248       Y4(I)=SPH(NN1,I)
          DO 249 I=1,NLEFT
          F1(I)=Y2(I)*Y3(I)+Y1(I)*Y4(I)
          F2(I)=Y1(I)*Y3(I)-Y2(I)*Y4(I)
          XX(I)=NN+MM*FACX(I)
249       SFAC(I)=S1(I)**MM
          DO 250 I=1,NLEFT
          IF(ABS(XX(I)).LT.AMUL)XX(I)=SIGN(AMUL,XX(I))
250       CONTINUE
          DO 252 K=1,NPO
```

```
      FK=K-1+0.5*MM
      DO 251 I=1,NLEFT
      AMN(I)=AMN(I)+XA(K,I)
251   AMNS(I)=AMNS(I)+XA(K,I)*FK
252   CONTINUE
      DO 253 I=1,NLEFT
      AMN(I)=AMN(I)*SFAC(I)
253   AMNS(I)=AMNS(I)*SFAC(I)/S(I)
      DO 254 I=1,NLEFT
      B2(I)=B2(I)+AMN(I)*F1(I)
      B2S(I)=B2S(I)+AMNS(I)*F1(I)
      B2PS(I)=B2PS(I)+AMN(I)*MM*F2(I)
254   B2PH(I)=B2PH(I)+AMN(I)*NN*F2(I)
      DO 255 I=1,NLEFT
      Y1(I)=AMN(I)*F1(I)*(MM*PCX(I)-NN*TCX(I))/(QTX(I)*XX(I))
255   Y2(I)=AMN(I)*F2(I)*FACZ(I)/XX(I)
      DO 256 I=1,NLEFT
      IF(MM.EQ.0.AND.NN.EQ.0) GO TO 256
      ALAM(I)=ALAM(I)+Y1(I)
      ZET(I)=ZET(I)-Y2(I)
256   CONTINUE
257   CONTINUE
258   IF(NUMD.EQ.0) GO TO 272
      DO 271 J=1,NUMD
      MM=MDB2(J)
      NPO=NPOL(MM)
      NN=NDB2(J)
      MM1=MD2(J)
      NN1=ND2(J)
      DO 259 I=1,NLEFT
      AMN(I)=0.0
259   AMNS(I)=0.0
      DO 261 K=1,NPO
      DO 260 I=1,NLEFT
260   XA(K,I)=XT(K,I)*B2D(J,K)
261   CONTINUE
      DO 262 I=1,NLEFT
      Y1(I)=CPS(MM1,I)
      Y2(I)=SPS(MM1,I)
      Y3(I)=CPH(NN1,I)
262   Y4(I)=SPH(NN1,I)
      DO 263 I=1,NLEFT
      F1(I)=Y2(I)*Y3(I)-Y1(I)*Y4(I)
      F2(I)=Y1(I)*Y3(I)+Y2(I)*Y4(I)
      XX(I)=NN-MM*FACX(I)
263   SFAC(I)=S1(I)**MM
      DO 264 I=1,NLEFT
      IF(ABS(XX(I)).LT.AMUL)XX(I)=SIGN(AMUL,XX(I))
264   CONTINUE
      DO 266 K=1,NPO
      FK=K-1+0.5*MM
      DO 265 I=1,NLEFT
      AMN(I)=AMN(I)+XA(K,I)
265   AMNS(I)=AMNS(I)+XA(K,I)*FK
266   CONTINUE
      DO 267 I=1,NLEFT
      AMN(I)=AMN(I)*SFAC(I)
267   AMNS(I)=AMNS(I)*SFAC(I)/S(I)
      DO 268 I=1,NLEFT
      B2(I)=B2(I)+AMN(I)*F1(I)
      B2S(I)=B2S(I)+AMNS(I)*F1(I)
```

```
         B2PS(I)=B2PS(I)+AMN(I)*MM*F2(I)
 268     B2PH(I)=B2PH(I)-AMN(I)*NN*F2(I)
         DO 269 I=1,NLEFT
         Y1(I)=AMN(I)*F1(I)*(MM*PCX(I)+NN*TCX(I))/(QTX(I)*XX(I))
 269     Y2(I)=AMN(I)*F2(I)*FACZ(I)/XX(I)
         DO 270 I=1,NLEFT
         IF(MM.EQ.0.AND.NN.EQ.0) GO TO 270
         ALAM(I)=ALAM(I)-Y1(I)
         ZET(I)=ZET(I)+Y2(I)
 270     CONTINUE
 271     CONTINUE
 272     CONTINUE
         DO 273 I=1,NLEFT
         ALAM(I)=ALAM(I)*PSX(I)+FACPX(I)
 273     ZET(I)=ZET(I)+ZTOX(I)
         DO 275 I=1,NLEFT
         B2MAX=AMAX1(B2MAX,B2(I))
         IF(B2MAX.NE.B2(I)) GO TO 274
         IB2MX=I
         SB2MX=S(I)
 274     CONTINUE
         B2MIN=AMIN1(B2MIN,B2(I))
         IF(B2MIN.NE.B2(I)) GO TO 275
         IB2MN=I
         SB2MN=S(I)
 275     CONTINUE
         DO 276 I=1,NLEFT
 276     B(I)=1.0/SQRT(ABS(B2(I)))
         DO 277 I=1,NLEFT
 277     Y1(I)=-0.5*B(I)*B(I)*B(I)
         DO 278 I=1,NLEFT
         BS(I)=Y1(I)*B2S(I)
         BPH(I)=Y1(I)*B2PH(I)
 278     BPS(I)=Y1(I)*B2PS(I)
         CALL ELPOT(Y)
         RETURN
C
 280     FORMAT(///,3X,"NEGATIVE S=",F6.3)
         END


         FUNCTION NPOL(M)
C        NUMBER OF TERMS IN INTERPOLATION
         USE NAME9
         NPOL=NP-(M+1)/2
         RETURN
         END


         SUBROUTINE ORBIT(NS,NPHI,NPSI,NMAG,NEKIN,FTAUE)
C        GUIDING CENTER DIFFERENTIAL EQUATIONS
         USE NAME1
         USE NAME2
         USE NAME3
         USE NAME5
         USE NAME6
         USE NAME7
         USE NAME9
         USE NAME11
         USE NAME12
         USE NAME13
```

165

```
      USE NAME14
      USE NAME15
      USE NAME17
      USE NAME18
      EXTERNAL FCN,GCN
      PRINT 35
      PRINT 38,(MO(J),NO(J),KO(J),J=1,NOFC)
      PRINT 40
      TSOL1=0.0
      CALL INIT(NS,NPHI,NPSI,NMAG,NEKIN)
      REWIND 4
      REWIND 3
      NPAR=NS*NPHI*NPSI
      NOR=NPAR*NMAG*NEKIN
      IO=50*IC
      DO 1 I=1,15
    1 FL(I)=-1.0
      X1=FLOAT(NLEFT)
      FACS=0.5*PI
      IF(NSTU.LE.0) GO TO 4
      REWIND 4
      DO  2 I=1,20000
      READ(4) (PL(I,J),J=1,10)
      IF(PL(I,1).LT.0.0) GO TO  3
    2 CONTINUE
    3 READ (4) T1,T2,TSE1,NODE,NLEFT,ICOL,NOR,NTER,KTER,INI
      READ (4) (ETA(KK),AMAG(KK),SO(KK),PSIO(KK),PHIO(KK),SJ(KK),TJ(KK)
     1 ,ETA0(KK),ETAMA(KK),ETAMI(KK),PSIT(KK),PHIT(KK),B(KK),
     2 Y(4*KK-3),Y(4*KK-2),Y(4*KK-1),Y(4*KK),EKINO(KK),EKIN(KK),
     3 POT(KK),EKMAX(KK),EKMIN(KK),ENER(KK),KK=1,NOR)
      TSOL1=T2/1000000.
      GO TO 8
    4 CONTINUE
      NLOST=0
      NLEFT=NOR
      DO 5 KK=1,NOR
      TJ(KK)=0.0
      SJ(KK)=0.0
      ETA(KK)=ETA0(KK)
      ETAMA(KK)=ETA(KK)
      ETAMI(KK)=ETA(KK)
      EKIN(KK)=EKINO(KK)
      EKMAX(KK)=EKINO(KK)
      EKMIN(KK)=EKINO(KK)
      Y(4*KK-3)=SO(KK)
      Y(4*KK-2)=PSIO(KK)*PI2
    5 Y(4*KK-1)=PHIO(KK)*PI2
      CALL BVAL(Y)
      DO 6 KK=1,NOR
      ENER(KK)=EKIN(KK)+POT(KK)*IEL
      Y(4*KK)=SQRT(2.0*EKIN(KK))*ETA(KK)/B(KK)
    6 AMAG(KK)=EKIN(KK)*(1.0-ETA(KK)*ETA(KK))/B(KK)
      NTER=1000
      KTER=0
      INI=0
      T1=0.0
      T2=0.0
      CALL EVAL(T2,Y,NOR)
      TSOL1=0.0
      TEAVO=TEAV
      X1=FLOAT(NLEFT)
```

```
       WRITE (3) TEMAX,TEMIN,DENER,X1,FAV,GAV,PAV,TEAV,ETDV,TSOL1
    8  CONTINUE
       T2=T2+SDELT
       DO  9 NN=1,NCOL
       CALL COLL(NLEFT,FTAU,FTAUE,Y)
       ICOL=ICOL+1
    9  CONTINUE
       DO 10 KK=1,NLEFT
       IF(EKIN(KK).LT.0.04*EC) EKIN(KK)=0.04*EC
       Y(4*KK-3)=AMAX1(0.05,Y(4*KK-3))
   10  CONTINUE
       CALL BVAL(Y)
       DO 11 KK=1,NLEFT
       ENER(KK)=EKIN(KK)+POT(KK)*IEL
       Y(4*KK)=SQRT(2.0*EKIN(KK))*ETA(KK)/B(KK)
   11  AMAG(KK)=EKIN(KK)*(1.0-ETA(KK)*ETA(KK))/B(KK)
       IFAIL=1
       TOL=10**(-ACC)*RADL
       HMAX=0.0
       NODE=NLEFT*4
C      ADAMS INTEGRATION OF ODE
       CALL D02CHF(T1,T2,NODE,Y,TOL,1,HMAX,FCN,GCN,WORK,IFAIL)
       T2=T1
       TSOL1=T2/1000000
       CALL EVAL(T2,Y,NOR)
       NTER=NTER+1
       KTER=KTER+1
       IF(KTER.GE.IO) GO TO 13
   12  GO TO 14
   13  KTER=0
   14  CONTINUE
       X1=FLOAT(NLEFT)
C      SAVE ORBIT DATA
       WRITE (3) TEMAX,TEMIN,DENER,X1,FAV,GAV,PAV,TEAV,ETDV,TSOL1
       IF(NTER.LT.IC) GO TO 15
       NTER=0
       IF(KOUNT.GT.0) PRINT 39,TSOL1,(FC(J),J=1,NOFC)
   15  CALL SECOND(TIM1)
       IF(TIM1.GE.TLIM) GO TO 27
   20  IF (IFAIL.EQ.0.OR.IFAIL.EQ.4) GO TO 21
       PRINT 31,IFAIL
       GO TO 25
   21  IF(TOL.GT.0.0) GO TO 25
       PRINT 32,TOL
   25  IF(NLEFT.EQ.0) GO TO 29
   26  IF(T2.LT.TSE) GO TO 8
   27  CONTINUE
       DO 28 KK=1,NLEFT
       TJ(KK)=T2/1000000
       PSIT(KK)=Y(4*KK-2)
       PHIT(KK)=Y(4*KK-1)
   28  SJ(KK)=Y(4*KK-3)
   29  WRITE (3) (FL(I),I=1,10)
       WRITE (3) T1,T2,TSE,NODE,NLEFT,ICOL,NOR,NTER,KTER,INI
       WRITE (3) (ETA(KK),AMAG(KK),S0(KK),PSI0(KK),PHI0(KK),SJ(KK),TJ(KK)
      1 ,ETA0(KK),ETAMA(KK),ETAMI(KK),PSIT(KK),PHIT(KK),B(KK),
      2 Y(4*KK-3),Y(4*KK-2),Y(4*KK-1),Y(4*KK),EKIN0(KK),EKIN(KK),
      3 POT(KK),EKMAX(KK),EKMIN(KK),ENER(KK),KK=1,NOR)
       DO 30 JC=1,NOR
       YC(4*JC-3)=Y(4*JC-3)
       YC(4*JC-2)=Y(4*JC-2)
```

```
          YC(4*JC-1)=Y(4*JC-1)
          YC(4*JC)=Y(4*JC)
   30     CONTINUE
          RADF=RADL*SQRT(TEAVF/TEAV0)
          PRINT 41, RADF
          RETURN
C
   31     FORMAT(///,3X,"IFAIL=",I2)
   32     FORMAT(///,3X,"NEGATIVE TOL=",F8.3)
   35     FORMAT(//////)
   36     FORMAT(2X,5F10.3,E13.3,3F10.3,3X,I5)
   37     FORMAT(///,8X,"TIME",6X,"AV E",5X,"E MAX",5X,"E MIN",3X,
         1 "DEV ETA",6X,"ENERCON",7X,"FAV",7X,"GAV",7X," 1",3X,"NLEFT"///)
   38     FORMAT(///15X,"FOURIER COEFFICIENTS OF DISTRIBUTION FUNCTION",///
         1 ,25X,"(S**K/2)*COS(M*PSI-N*PHI)",//
         2 ,6X,"TIME",2X,6(I2,1H,,I3,1H,,I1,2X))
   39     FORMAT(2X,F8.3,5X,6(F5.3,5X))
   40     FORMAT(/)
   41     FORMAT(//,5X,12HFINAL RADL =F8.5)
          END


          SUBROUTINE EVAL(TIM,Y,NOR)
C         EXPONENTIAL DECAY FUNCTIONALS
          USE NAME2
          USE NAME3
          USE NAME9
          USE NAME10
          USE NAME11
          USE NAME12
          USE NAME13
          USE NAME14
          USE NAME18
          IF(T2.GE.0.5*TSE)KOUNT=KOUNT+1
          NL=NLEFT
          I=0
    1     IF(I.EQ.NL) GO TO 2
          I=I+1
          IF(Y(4*I-3).LT.0.98) GO TO 1
          I4=4*I
          NL4=4*NL
          X1=Y(I4-3)
          X2=Y(I4-2)
          X3=Y(I4-1)
          X4=Y(I4)
          X5=ETA(I)
          X6=AMAG(I)
          X7=S0(I)
          X8=PSI0(I)
          X9=PHI0(I)
          X10=ETA0(I)
          X11=ETAMA(I)
          X12=ETAMI(I)
          X13=EKIN0(I)
          X14=EKMAX(I)
          X15=EKMIN(I)
          X16=EKIN(I)
          X17=ENER(I)
          X18=POT(I)
          Y(I4-3)=Y(NL4-3)
          Y(I4-2)=Y(NL4-2)
```

```
      Y(I4-1)=Y(NL4-1)
      Y(I4)=Y(NL4)
      ETA(I)=ETA(NL)
      AMAG(I)=AMAG(NL)
      SO(I)=SO(NL)
      TJ(I)=TJ(NL)
      SJ(I)=SJ(NL)
      PSIT(I)=PSIT(NL)
      PHIT(I)=PHIT(NL)
      PSIO(I)=PSIO(NL)
      PHIO(I)=PHIO(NL)
      ETAO(I)=ETAO(NL)
      ETAMA(I)=ETAMA(NL)
      ETAMI(I)=ETAMI(NL)
      EKINO(I)=EKINO(NL)
      EKMAX(I)=EKMAX(NL)
      EKMIN(I)=EKMIN(NL)
      EKIN(I)=EKIN(NL)
      ENER(I)=ENER(NL)
      POT(I)=POT(NL)
      Y(NL4-3)=1.0
      Y(NL4-2)=X2
      Y(NL4-1)=X3
      Y(NL4)=X4
      ETA(NL)=X5
      AMAG(NL)=X6
      PSIT(NL)=X2
      PHIT(NL)=X3
      TJ(NL)=TIM/1000000
      SJ(NL)=0.999999
      SO(NL)=X7
      PSIO(NL)=X8
      PHIO(NL)=X9
      ETAO(NL)=X10
      ETAMA(NL)=X11
      ETAMI(NL)=X12
      EKINO(NL)=X13
      EKMAX(NL)=X14
      EKMIN(NL)=X15
      EKIN(NL)=X16
      ENER(NL)=X17
      POT(NL)=X18
      NL=NL-1
      I=I-1
      GO TO 1
2     NLEFT=NL
      IF(NLEFT.EQ.0) RETURN
      CALL BVAL(Y)
      DO 3 I=1,NLEFT
3     EKIN(I)=B(I)*(AMAG(I)+0.5*B(I)*Y(4*I)*Y(4*I))
      DO 4 KK=1,NLEFT
4     Y3(KK)=EKIN(KK)/EC
      DO  5 KK=1,NLEFT
      ETA(KK)=Y(4*KK)*B(KK)/SQRT(2.0*EKIN(KK))
      IF(ABS(ETA(KK)).GT.1.) ETA(KK)=ETA(KK)/(ABS(ETA(KK))+1.0E-14)
5     CONTINUE
      DO 11 I=1,NLEFT
11    Y2(I)=EKIN(I)+IEL*POT(I)
      SAV=0.0
      X1=0.0
      GAV=0.0
```

```
      PAV=0.0
      ETAV=0.0
      TEAV=0.0
      TEMAX=0.0
      TEMIN=1000000.0
      DO 12 I=1,NLEFT
      TEAV=TEAV+Y3(I)
      TEMAX=AMAX1(TEMAX,Y3(I))
      TEMIN=AMIN1(TEMIN,Y3(I))
      GAV=GAV+(1.-SO(I))*COS(FACS*(Y(4*I-3)-SO(I)))/(1.-Y(4*I-3)*SO(I)))
     1 /NOR
      ETAV=ETAV+ETA(I)
      SAV=SAV+Y(4*I-3)
   12 X1=X1+(Y2(I)-ENER(I))*(Y2(I)-ENER(I))
      FAV=2.0*(NLEFT-SAV)/FLOAT(NOR)
      SAV=SAV/FLOAT(NLEFT)
      ETAV=ETAV/FLOAT(NLEFT)
      TEAV=TEAV/FLOAT(NOR)
      DENER=SQRT(X1/NLEFT)/EC
      SDV=0.0
      DO 13 I=1,NLEFT
   13 SDV=SDV+(Y(4*I-3)-SAV)*(Y(4*I-3)-SAV)
      SDV=SQRT(SDV/NLEFT)
      ETDV=0.0
      DO 14 I=1,NLEFT
      EKMAX(I)=AMAX1(EKMAX(I),Y3(I))
      EKMIN(I)=AMIN1(EKMIN(I),Y3(I))
      ETAMA(I)=AMAX1(ETAMA(I),ETA(I))
      ETAMI(I)=AMIN1(ETAMI(I),ETA(I))
   14 ETDV=ETDV+(ETAMA(I)-ETAMI(I))
      ETDV=ETDV/FLOAT(NLEFT)
      NLOST=NOR-NLEFT
      PAV=FLOAT(NLEFT)/FLOAT(NOR)
      IF (KOUNT. EQ. 0) GO TO 20
C     THE FOURIER COEFFICIENTS OF THE DISTRIBUTION FUNCTION ARE
C     CODED HERE. THEY SHOULD BE CORRELATED WITH THE CODING IN
C     SUBROUTINE ELPOT.
      DO 19 J=1,NOFC
      FT=0.
      X1=0.5*KO(J)
      DO 18 I=1,NLEFT
   18 FT=FT+(Y(4*I-3)**X1)*COS(MO(J)*Y(4*I-2)-NO(J)*Y(4*I-1))/
     1 FLOAT(NLEFT)
   19 FC(J)=(FC(J)*FLOAT(KOUNT-1)+1.0*(FLOAT(KO(J))+2.)*FT)
     1 /FLOAT(KOUNT)
      TEAVF=(TEAVF*FLOAT(KOUNT-1)+TEAV)/FLOAT(KOUNT)
   20 CONTINUE
      RETURN
      END


      SUBROUTINE COLL(NLEFT,FTAU,FTAUE,Y)
C     COLLISION OPERATOR
      USE NAME11
      USE NAME14
      DO 1 I=1,NLEFT
    1 PES4(I)=TEMP(Y(4*I-3))
      DO 2 I=1,NLEFT
    2 PES5(I)=1.0+(EKIN(I)/PES4(I))**1.5
      DO 3 I=1,NLEFT
      PES1(I)=RANF(1)-0.5
```

```
 3  PES2(I)=FTAU*(1.0-ETA(I)*ETA(I))/PES5(I)
    DO 4 I=1,NLEFT
 4  PES3(I)=SIGN(1.0,PES1(I))
    DO 5 I=1,NLEFT
 5  ETA(I)=PES3(I)*SQRT(PES2(I))+(1.0-FTAU/PES5(I))*ETA(I)
    DO 7 I=1,NLEFT
    PES1(I)=RANF(1)-0.5
    PES2(I)=1.5*PES4(I)/PES5(I)
 7  PES3(I)=PES4(I)*EKIN(I)*FTAUE/PES5(I)
    DO 9 I=1,NLEFT
 9  EKIN(I)=EKIN(I)+2.*SIGN(1.0,PES1(I))*SQRT(PES3(I))-2.0*FTAUE*(EKIN
   1 (I)-PES2(I))/PES5(I)
    RETURN
    END


    FUNCTION GCN(T,Y)
C   CRITERION FOR ODE SOLVER
    USE NAME9
    USE NAME11
    USE NAME12
    USE NAME14
    DO 1 I=1,NLEFT
 1  PES1(I)=Y(4*I-3)
    X1=0.0
    DO 2 I=1,NLEFT
 2  X1=AMAX1(X1,PES1(I))
    GCN=1.0-X1
    RETURN
    END


    SUBROUTINE FCN(T,Y,F)
C   RIGHT HAND SIDE OF ODE
    USE NAME9
    USE NAME11
    USE NAME14
    USE NAME12
    USE NAME13
    CALL BVAL(Y)
    DO 1 I=1,NLEFT
 1  Y1(I)=Y(4*I)*Y(4*I)
    DO 2 I=1,NLEFT
    Y2(I)=AMAG(I)+B(I)*Y1(I)
 2  Y3(I)=-PI2/(QTX(I)*PCX(I)+QX(I)*TCX(I))
    DO 3 I=1,NLEFT
    Y4(I)=PI2*ZET(I)*Y2(I)
    PES1(I)=PCX(I)*BPS(I)-TCX(I)*BPH(I)
 3  B2(I)=B(I)*B(I)
    DO 4 I=1,NLEFT
    PES4(I)=PCX(I)*POTPS(I)-TCX(I)*POTPH(I)
    PES5(I)=QX(I)*POTPS(I)+QTX(I)*POTPH(I)
    PES6(I)=Y(4*I)*PSX(I)/B2(I)
    PES2(I)=PSX(I)*Y1(I)+BS(I)*Y2(I)
 4  PES3(I)=1.0+IEL*ALAM(I)*Y(4*I)
    DO 5 I=1,NLEFT
    F1(I)=-Y3(I)*(Y2(I)*PES1(I)*IEL+PES4(I))
 5  F2(I)=Y3(I)*(-Y(4*I)*B2(I)*QX(I)*PES3(I)+(PCX(I)*PES2(I)
   1 -Y4(I)*BPH(I))*IEL+PCX(I)*POTS(I)-PI2*ZET(I)*POTPH(I))
    DO 14 I=1,NLEFT
14  F(4*I-3)=F1(I)
```

171

```
      DO 15 I=1,NLEFT
   15 F(4*I-2)=F2(I)
      DO 16 I=1,NLEFT
      F1(I)=Y3(I)*(-Y(4*I)*B2(I)*QTX(I)*PES3(I)-(TCX(I)*PES2(I)
     1 -Y4(I)*BPS(I))*IEL-TCX(I)*POTS(I)+PI2*ZET(I)*POTPS(I))
   16 F2(I)=-Y3(I)*(Y2(I)*(-PES3(I)*(QX(I)*BPS(I)+QTX(I)*BPH(I))
     1 +PES6(I)*PES1(I)*IEL)-PES3(I)*PES5(I)*IEL+PES4(I)*PES6(I))
      DO 17 I=1,NLEFT
   17 F(4*I-1)=F1(I)
      DO 18 I=1,NLEFT
   18 F(4*I)=F2(I)
      RETURN
      END


      SUBROUTINE INIT(NS,NPHI,NPSI,NMAG,NEKIN)
C     INITIALIZATION OF VARIABLES
      USE NAME2
      USE NAME9
      HU=1.0/NPSI
      HV=1.0/NPHI
      HETA=2.0/NMAG
      SUM=0.0
      HS=1.0/50.0
      DO 3 I=1,50
      S=(I-0.5)*HS
      X2=2.0*(1.0-S)
    3 SUM=SUM+HS*X2*(1.0-TE1*S**NTE1)**NTE2
      T0=2.0*EC/(3.0*SUM)
      DO 5 I=1,NS
      X1=(2.*FLOAT(I)-1.)/(2.*FLOAT(NS))
      X2=1.0-SQRT(X1)
      TS=TEMP(X2)
      DO 5 M=1,NEKIN
      CALL ENIN(NEKIN,XX,M)
      X2=TS*XX*XX
      DO 5 J=1,NPHI
      DO 5 K=1,NPSI
      DO 5 L=1,NMAG
      KK=I+NS*(J-1+NPHI*(K-1+NPSI*(L-1+NMAG*(M-1))))
      EKINO(KK)=X2
      SO(KK)=1.0-SQRT(X1)
      PHIO(KK)=HV*(J-1.0)
      PSIO(KK)=HU*(K-1.0)
      ETA0(KK)= -1.0+HETA*(L-0.5)
    5 AMAGO(KK)=1.0-ETA0(KK)*ETA0(KK)
      RETURN
      END


      SUBROUTINE ENIN(N,XX,M)
C     ENERGY INITIALIZATION
      PI=3.1415926536
      X1=SQRT(PI)/(4.0*N)
      DO 1 I=1,100
      X=0.1*I
      F=-0.5*X*EXP(-X*X)+0.5*ERF(X)-(M-0.5)*X1
      IF(F.GT.0.0) GO TO 2
    1 CONTINUE
    2 CONTINUE
      IT=0
```

```
  3  F=-0.5*X*EXP(-X*X)+0.5*ERF(X)-(M-0.5)*X1
     FP=X*X*EXP(-X*X)
     DELX=-F/FP
     IT=IT+1
     IF(IT.GT.20) GO TO 4
     X=X+DELX
     IF(ABS(DELX).GT.0.0001) GO TO 3
     XX=X
     RETURN
  4  PRINT 5,IT,DELX
     STOP
C
  5  FORMAT(//,3X,"ENERGY INITIALIZATION DOES NOT CONVERGE",
    1 3X,I2,3X,E10.2)
     END



     FUNCTION ERF(X)
C    ERROR FUNCTION
     ERF=0.0
     DX=X/50.0
     DO 1 I=1,50
     X1=(I-0.5)*DX
  1  ERF=ERF+EXP(-X1*X1)*DX
     RETURN
     END



     FUNCTION TEMP(S)
C    TEMPERATURE PROFILE
     USE NAME2
     USE NAME9
     TEMP=T0*(1.0-TE1*S**NTE1)**NTE2
     RETURN
     END



     FUNCTION BNORM (I1,I2,X,F,XX1,XX2)
C    COMPUTES L2 NORM
     DIMENSION X(101), F(101)
     IN=I1
     IEND=I2
     XIN=XX1*XX1
     XEND=XX2*XX2
     BNORM=0.0
     IEND1=IEND-1
     DO 10 I=IN,IEND1
     X1=(X(I+1)-X(I))*0.5*(F(I)*F(I)+F(I+1)*F(I+1))
 10  BNORM=BNORM+X1
     BNORM=BNORM/(XEND-XIN)
     BNORM=SQRT(BNORM)
     RETURN
     END



     SUBROUTINE SPLIF (M,N,S,F,FP,FPP,FPPP,KM,VM,KN,VN,MODE,FQM,IND)
C    GENERAL PURPOSE CUBIC SPLINE FIT
     DIMENSION S(1), F(1), FP(1), FPP(1), FPPP(1)
     IND=0
     K=IABS(N-M)
     IF (K-1) 180,180,10
```

173

```
 10   K=(N-M)/K
      I=M
      J=M+K
      DS=S(J)-S(I)
      D=DS
      IF (DS) 20,180,20
 20   DF=(F(J)-F(I))/DS
      IF (KM-2) 30,40,50
 30   U=.5
      V=3.*(DF-VM)/DS
      GO TO 80
 40   U=0.
      V=VM
      GO TO 80
 50   U=-1.
      V=-DS*VM
      GO TO 80
 60   I=J
      J=J+K
      DS=S(J)-S(I)
      IF (D*DS) 180,180,70
 70   DF=(F(J)-F(I))/DS
      B=1./(DS+DS+U)
      U=B*DS
      V=B*(6.*DF-V)
 80   FP(I)=U
      FPP(I)=V
      U=(2.-U)*DS
      V=6.*DF+DS*V
      IF (J-N) 60,90,60
 90   IF (KN-2) 100,110,120
100   V=(6.*VN-V)/U
      GO TO 130
110   V=VN
      GO TO 130
120   V=(DS*VN+FPP(I))/(1.+FP(I))
130   B=V
      D=DS
140   DS=S(J)-S(I)
      U=FPP(I)-FP(I)*V
      FPPP(I)=(V-U)/DS
      FPP(I)=U
      FP(I)=(F(J)-F(I))/DS-DS*(V+U+U)/6.
      V=U
      J=I
      I=I-K
      IF (J-M) 140,150,140
150   I=N-K
      FPPP(N)=FPPP(I)
      FPP(N)=B
      FP(N)=DF+D*(FPP(I)+B+B)/6.
      IND=1
      IF (MODE) 180,180,160
160   FPPP(J)=FQM
      V=FPP(J)
170   I=J
      J=J+K
      DS=S(J)-S(I)
      U=FPP(J)
      FPPP(J)=FPPP(I)+.5*DS*(F(I)+F(J)-DS*DS*(U+V)/12.)
      V=U
```

```
      IF (J-N) 170,180,170
  180 RETURN
      END


      SUBROUTINE INTPL (MI,NI,SI,FI,M,N,S,F,FP,FPP,FPPP,MODE)
C     GENERAL PURPOSE INTERPOLATION USING TAYLOR SERIES
      DIMENSION SI(1), FI(1), S(1), F(1), FP(1), FPP(1), FPPP(1)
      K=IABS(N-M)
      K=(N-M)/K
      I=M
      MIN=MI
      NIN=NI
      D=S(N)-S(M)
      IF (D*(SI(NI)-SI(MI))) 10,20,20
   10 MIN=NI
      NIN=MI
   20 KI=IABS(NIN-MIN)
      IF (KI) 40,40,30
   30 KI=(NIN-MIN)/KI
   40 II=MIN-KI
      C=0.
      IF (MODE) 60,60,50
   50 C=1.
   60 II=II+KI
      SS=SI(II)
   70 I=I+K
      IF (I-N) 80,90,80
   80 IF (D*(S(I)-SS)) 70,70,90
   90 J=I
      I=I-K
      SS=SS-S(I)
      FPPPP=C*(FPPP(J)-FPPP(I))/(S(J)-S(I))
      FF=FPPP(I)+.25*SS*FPPPP
      FF=FPP(I)+SS*FF/3.
      FF=FP(I)+.5*SS*FF
      FI(II)=F(I)+SS*FF
      IF (II-NIN) 60,100,60
  100 RETURN
      END


      SUBROUTINE PINT (M,N,I1,I2,W,X,F,FX,C,SIG)
C     GENERAL PURPOSE POLYNOMIAL INTERPOLATION
      DIMENSION F(50), X(50), XW(50), A(10,10), B(10), C(10), AW(10,10),
     1 WKS1(10), WKS2(10), XK(50), XIK(50,6), FX(50)
      SIG=0.0
      NP=N
      AM=0.5*M
      DO 20 I=I1,I2
      XIK(I,1)=X(I)**AM
      DO 10 J=2,NP
   10 XIK(I,J)=XIK(I,J-1)*X(I)
   20 XW(I)=ABS(X(I))**W
      DO 50 K=1,NP
      B(K)=0.0
      DO 30 I=I1,I2
   30 B(K)=B(K)+XW(I)*F(I)*XIK(I,K)
      DO 40 J=1,NP
      A(K,J)=0.0
      DO 40 I=I1,I2
```

175

```
   40  A(K,J)=A(K,J)+XW(I)*XIK(I,K)*XIK(I,J)
   50  CONTINUE
       CALL F04ATF (A,10,B,NP,C,AW,10,WKS1,WKS2,IFAIL)
       IF (IFAIL.EQ.0) GO TO 60
       PRINT 90, IFAIL
   60  SUM=0.0
       DO 80 I=I1,I2
       SUM=SUM+XW(I)
       FX(I)=0.0
       DO 70 K=1,NP
   70  FX(I)=FX(I)+C(K)*XIK(I,K)
       FB=FX(I)-F(I)
   80  SIG=SIG+XW(I)*FB*FB
       SIG=SQRT(SIG/SUM)
       RETURN
C
   90  FORMAT (//,3X,"IFAIL=",I5,//)
       END


       SUBROUTINE FPRINT
C      PRINTS FINAL RESULTS
       USE NAME2
       USE NAME3
       USE NAME5
       USE NAME6
       USE NAME9
       USE NAME11
       IF(NPRT.LT.0) GO TO 20
       PRINT 200
       DO 10 J=1,NOR
       X1=EKIN(J)/EC
       X2=EKIN0(J)/EC
   10  PRINT 210,J,TJ(J),SJ(J),ETA(J),X1,PHI0(J),PSI0(J),ETA0(J),X2
   20  CONTINUE
       NTOT=NOR-NLOST
       PRINT 220,NLOST,NTOT
       RETURN
C
  200  FORMAT(//,8X,"NUMBER",9X,"T",9X,"S",7X,"ETA",6X,"T/EC",6X,"PHI0",
      1 6X,"PSI0",6X,"ETA0",5X,"T0/EC",//)
  210  FORMAT(11X,I3,8(4X,F6.3))
  220  FORMAT(//,9X,"NUMBER LOST =",I5,12X,"NUMBER REMAINING =",I6/)
       END


       SUBROUTINE TPLOT(Y)
C      COMPUTES AND PLOTS LOSS RATES
       USE NAME2
       USE NAME3
       USE NAME6
       USE NAME9
       USE NAME11
       USE NAME12
       USE NAME13
       USE NAME14
       USE NAME15
       DIMENSION TAU1(5),TAU2(5),TAU3(5),DEV1(5),DEV2(5),DEV3(5),EX1(5),
      1 EX2(5),EX3(5),TINT(5),TEXTX(3),TEXTY(3),SYM(4),DENP(100),
      2 DENL(100),XDEN(100)
       DO 1 I=1,15
```

```
1   FL(I)=-1.0
    IK2=0
    REWIND 3
    CALL KEEP80 (1,3)
    CALL FR80ID
    CALL MAP(0.0,14.0,0.0,12.0)
    IENDM=0
    IF(NSTU.LE.0) GO TO 4
    REWIND 4
    DO 2 I=1,7000
    READ (4) (PL(I,J),J=1,10)
    IEND=I
    IF (PL(I,1).LT.0.) GO TO 3
2   CONTINUE
3   IEND=IEND-1
    IK=IEND
    IK2=IK
4   CONTINUE
    REWIND 3
    DO 6 I=1,7000
    IK2=IK2+1
    READ (3) (PL(IK2,J),J=1,10)
    IF(PL(IK2,1).LT.0.0) GO TO 7
6   CONTINUE
7   IK2=IK2-1
8   IEND=IK2
    IF(NSTU.LE.0) GO TO 10
    REWIND 3
    DO 9 I=1,IEND
    WRITE (3) (PL(I,J),J=1,10)
9   CONTINUE
    WRITE (3) (FL(I),I=1,10)
    WRITE (3) T1,T2,TSE,NODE,NLEFT,ICOL,NOR,NTER,KTER,INI
    WRITE (3) (ETA(KK),AMAG(KK),SO(KK),PSIO(KK),PHIO(KK),SJ(KK),TJ(KK)
   1 ,ETAO(KK),ETAMA(KK),ETAMI(KK),PSIT(KK),PHIT(KK),B(KK),
   2 Y(4*KK-3),Y(4*KK-2),Y(4*KK-1),Y(4*KK),EKINO(KK),EKIN(KK),
   3 POT(KK),EKMAX(KK),EKMIN(KK),ENER(KK),KK=1,NOR)
10  IF(NSTU.LT.0) CALL ADDORB
    XD=1.5
    YD=8.0
    IN(5)=10
    IENDM=MAXO(IENDM,IEND)
    IF(IEND.GT.7000) IEND=7000
    TEXTX(1)=8H
    TEXTX(2)=8HTIME
    TEXTX(3)=8H
    IF(NPRT.LT.0) GO TO 17
    CALL SETLCH(5.0,11.5,1,0,1,0)
    WRITE(100,530)
    TEXTY(1)=8H     MAX
    TEXTY(2)=8HTEMP
    TEXTY(3)=8H
    DO 16 I=1,4
16  SYM(I)=8H
    IN(1)=1
    CALL PLOTB(4.,2.,IEND,1,TEXTX,TEXTY,SYM,XD,YD)
    YD=YD-3.5
    TEXTY(1)=8H     MIN
    IN(1)=2
    CALL PLOTB(4.,2.,IEND,1,TEXTX,TEXTY,SYM,XD,YD)
    YD=YD-3.5
```

177

```
      TEXTY(1)=8HAVERAGE
      IN(1)=8
      CALL PLOTB(4.,2.,IEND,1,TEXTX,TEXTY,SYM,XD,YD)
      XD=XD+7.2
      YD=YD+7.0
      TEXTY(1)=8HPARTICLE
      TEXTY(2)=8HS REMAIN
      TEXTY(3)=8H
      IN(1)=4
      CALL PLOTB(4.,2.,IEND,1,TEXTX,TEXTY,SYM,XD,YD)
      YD=YD-3.5
      TEXTY(1)=8HDEVIATIO
      TEXTY(2)=8HN ETA
      IN(1)=9
      CALL PLOTB(4.,2.,IEND,1,TEXTX,TEXTY,SYM,XD,YD)
      YD=YD-3.5
      TEXTY(1)=8H  ENERCO
      TEXTY(2)=8HN
      IN(1)=3
      CALL PLOTB(4.,2.,IEND,1,TEXTX,TEXTY,SYM,XD,YD)
      CALL FRAME
17    CONTINUE
      CALL SETLCH(4.50,11.0,1,0,1,0)
      WRITE(100,540)
      XD=6.0
      YD=7.75
      TEXTY(1)=8H  LOG (1
      TEXTY(2)=8H-S)
      TEXTY(3)=8H
      IN(1)=5
      NTER=1000
      NIC1=INT(1.0/(SDELT*SFREQ))
      COLT=1.0/(SFREQ*100000)
      IL=IEND
      DO  18 I=1,IL
      PL(I,1)=PL(I,5)
      PL(I,2)=PL(I,6)
      PL(I,9)=PL(I,7)
18    CONTINUE
      DO 20 I=1,IEND
      NTER=NTER+1
      PL(I,5)=ALOG(PL(I,5))
      PL(I,6)=ALOG(PL(I,6))
      PL(I,7)=ALOG(PL(I,7))
      IC1=1+IC/4
      IF(NTER.LT.IC1) GO TO 20
      NTER=0
      NL=NOR-ABS(PL(I,4))
20    CONTINUE
      IN2=IENDM-1
      I1=1+IENDM/10
      IN3=IENDM-I1
      DO 30 I=1,2
      CALL SLOPE(I1,IN3,5,EX1(I),DEV1(I))
      CALL SLOPE(I1,IN3,7,EX2(I),DEV2(I))
      CALL SLOPE(I1,IN3,6,EX3(I),DEV3(I))
      TINT(I)=(IN2-I1+1)*SDELT/1000000
      I1=(I1+IN2)/2
      IF(ABS(EX1(I)).LT.1.E-10) EX1(I)=1.E-10
      IF(ABS(EX2(I)).LT.1.E-10) EX2(I)=1.E-10
      IF(ABS(EX3(I)).LT.1.E-10) EX3(I)=1.E-10
```

178

```
      TAU1(I)=1.0/EX1(I)
      TAU2(I)=1.0/EX2(I)
      TAU3(I)=1.0/EX3(I)
      IF(TAU3(I).LT.0.0001) TAU3(I)=0.0001
30    CONTINUE
      TINTF=10.*TINT(1)
      TAUF=10.*TAU3(2)
      XMAX=0.
      DO 40 I=1,NOR
      XMAX=AMAX1(XMAX,ABS(PHIT(I))/PI2)
40    CONTINUE
      XMEAN=XMAX*COLT/TINTF
      PRINT 330,COLT,XMAX
      ITIMF=AINT(TIMF)
      PRINT 490,PL(IL,3),ITIMF
      PRINT 500,XMEAN
      CALL PLOTB(4.,2.,IN2,1,TEXTX,TEXTY,SYM,XD,YD)
      IF(NPRT.LT.0) GO TO 43
      YD=YD-3.5
      IN(1)=7
      TEXTY(1)=8H    LOG
      TEXTY(2)=8HNLEFT
      CALL PLOTB(4.,2.,IN2,1,TEXTX,TEXTY,SYM,XD,YD)
43    CONTINUE
      YD=YD-3.5
      IN(1)=6
      TEXTY(1)=8H    LOG C
      TEXTY(2)=8HOS
      CALL PLOTB(4.,2.,IN2,1,TEXTX,TEXTY,SYM,XD,YD)
      NIC1=INT(1.0/(SDELT*SFREQ))
      NIC2=NIC1/2
      PRINT 440
      IF(IEL.LT.0) GO TO 51
      MSTAU=AINT(TAUF)
      PRINT 510,MSTAU,MSTAU
      GO TO 60
51    TAUF=TAUF/(43.*43.)
      MSTAU=AINT(TAUF)
      PRINT 520,MSTAU,MSTAU
      DO 52 I=1,2
      TAU1(I)=TAU1(I)/(43.*43.)
      TAU2(I)=TAU2(I)/(43.*43.)
      TAU3(I)=TAU3(I)/(43.*43.)
      EX1(I)=EX1(I)*(43.*43.)
      EX2(I)=EX2(I)*(43.*43.)
      EX3(I)=EX3(I)*(43.*43.)
52    CONTINUE
60    IF(NIC1.LE.IN2) GO TO 70
      NIC1=NIC2
      NIC2=NIC1/2
      GO TO 60
70    CONTINUE
      PRINT 420
      PRINT 430
      PRINT 450
      TINT(1)=10.*TINT(1)
      TINT(2)=10.*TINT(2)
      TAU1(1)=10.*TAU1(1)
      TAU1(2)=10.*TAU1(2)
      EX1(1)=0.1*EX1(1)
      EX1(2)=0.1*EX1(2)
```

```
      PRINT 470,TINT(1),TAU1(1),EX1(1),DEV1(1)
      PRINT 460,TINT(2),TAU1(2),EX1(2),DEV1(2)
      PRINT 410
      PRINT 430
      PRINT 450
      DO 80 I=1,2
      TAU3(I)=10.*TAU3(I)
      EX3(I)=0.1*EX3(I)
      TAU2(I)=10.*TAU2(I)
      EX2(I)=0.1*EX2(I)
   80 CONTINUE
      PRINT 470,TINT(1),TAU3(1),EX3(1),DEV3(1)
      PRINT 460,TINT(2),TAU3(2),EX3(2),DEV3(2)
      PRINT 480
      PRINT 430
      PRINT 450
      PRINT 470,TINT(1),TAU2(1),EX2(1),DEV2(1)
      PRINT 460,TINT(2),TAU2(2),EX2(2),DEV2(2)
C     HISTOGRAMS
      NINT=20
      NINT2=2*NINT+1
      NINT3=2*NINT
      CALL DENSITY(NINT,NLEFT,NOR,SO,XDEN,DENP,DENL,-1)
      IF(NPRT.LT.0) GO TO 90
      PRINT 340,(XDEN(I),I=1,NINT3,2)
      PRINT 350,(DENP(I),I=1,NINT3,2)
   90 CONTINUE
      DO 100 I=1,NINT2
      PL(I,4)=XDEN(I)
  100 PL(I,5)=DENP(I)
      CALL FRAME
      CALL SETLCH(6.0,11.,1,0,1,0)
      WRITE(100,550)
      XD=1.5
      YD=8.0
      TEXTX(1)=8H
      TEXTX(2)=8H     S
      TEXTX(3)=8H
      TEXTY(1)=8H   INITI
      TEXTY(2)=8HAL
      TEXTY(3)=8H
      IN(1)=5
      IN(5)=4
      IN(2)=6
      CALL PLOTB(4.,2.,NINT2,1,TEXTX,TEXTY,SYM,XD,YD)
      CALL DENSITY(NINT,NLEFT,NOR,SJ,XDEN,DENP,DENL,1)
      IF(NPRT.LT.0) GO TO 102
      PRINT 370,(XDEN(I),I=1,NINT3,2)
      PRINT 350,(DENP(I),I=1,NINT3,2)
      PRINT 360,(DENL(I),I=1,NINT3,2)
  102 CONTINUE
      DO 103 I=1,NINT2
      PL(I,4)=XDEN(I)
  103 PL(I,5)=DENP(I)
      TEXTY(1)=8H   FINAL
      TEXTY(2)=8H
      YD=YD-3.5
      CALL PLOTB(4.,2.,NINT2,1,TEXTX,TEXTY,SYM,XD,YD)
      XD=XD+7.2
      YD=YD+3.5
      CALL DENSITY(NINT,NLEFT,NOR,ETAO,XDEN,DENP,DENL,-1)
```

```
      IF(NPRT.LT.0) GO TO 104
      PRINT 380,(XDEN(I),I=1,NINT3,2)
      PRINT 350,(DENP(I),I=1,NINT3,2)
104   CONTINUE
      DO 105 I=1,NINT2
      PL(I,4)=XDEN(I)
105   PL(I,5)=DENP(I)
      TEXTX(1)=8H
      TEXTX(2)=8HETA
      TEXTY(1)=8H    INITI
      TEXTY(2)=8HAL
      CALL PLOTB(4.,2.,NINT2,1,TEXTX,TEXTY,SYM,XD,YD)
      CALL DENSITY(NINT,NLEFT,NOR,ETA,XDEN,DENP,DENL,1)
      IF(NPRT.LT.0) GO TO 106
      PRINT 390,(XDEN(I),I=1,NINT3,2)
      PRINT 350,(DENP(I),I=1,NINT3,2)
      PRINT 360,(DENL(I),I=1,NINT3,2)
106   CONTINUE
      DO 107 I=1,NINT2
      PL(I,6)=DENL(I)
      PL(I,4)=XDEN(I)
107   PL(I,5)=DENP(I)
      TEXTY(1)=8H  REMAIN
      TEXTY(2)=8HING
      YD=YD-3.5
      CALL PLOTB(4.,2.,NINT2,1,TEXTX,TEXTY,SYM,XD,YD)
      IN(1)=6
      YD=YD-3.5
      TEXTY(1)=8H     LOST
      TEXTY(2)=8H
      CALL PLOTB(4.,2.,NINT2,1,TEXTX,TEXTY,SYM,XD,YD)
      DO 108 I=1,NOR
      X1=PHIT(I)/PI2
      X2=PSIT(I)/PI2
      PES1(I)=AMOD(X1,1.0)
      PES2(I)=AMOD(X2,1.0)
      IF(PES1(I).LT.0.0) PES1(I)=PES1(I)+1.0
108   IF(PES2(I).LT.0.0) PES2(I)=PES2(I)+1.0
      CALL DENSITY(NINT,NLEFT,NOR,PHIO,XDEN,DENP,DENL,-1)
      IF(NPRT.LT.0) GO TO 109
      PRINT 400,(XDEN(I),I=1,NINT3,2)
      PRINT 350,(DENP(I),I=1,NINT3,2)
109   CONTINUE
      IF(NPRT.LT.0) GO TO 238
      CALL FRAME
      XD=1.5
      YD=8.0
      DO 118 I=1,NOR
      PES1(I)=EKINO(I)/EC
118   PES2(I)=EKIN(I)/EC
      CALL DENSITY(NINT,NLEFT,NOR,PES1,XDEN,DENP,DENL,-1)
      IF(NPRT.LT.0) GO TO 201
      PRINT 210,(XDEN(I),I=1,NINT3,2)
      PRINT 350,(DENP(I),I=1,NINT3,2)
201   CONTINUE
      DO 202 I=1,NINT2
      PL(I,4)=XDEN(I)
202   PL(I,5)=DENP(I)
      TEXTX(1)=8H
      TEXTX(2)=8HTEMP
      TEXTX(3)=8H
```

```
      TEXTY(1)=8H   INITI
      TEXTY(2)=8HAL
      TEXTY(3)=8H
      IN(1)=5
      IN(5)=4
      IN(2)=6
      CALL PLOTB(4.,2.,NINT2,1,TEXTX,TEXTY,SYM,XD,YD)
      CALL DENSITY(NINT,NLEFT,NOR,PES2,XDEN,DENP,DENL,1)
      IF(NPRT.LT.0) GO TO 203
      PRINT 211,(XDEN(I),I=1,NINT3,2)
      PRINT 350,(DENP(I),I=1,NINT3,2)
      PRINT 360,(DENL(I),I=1,NINT3,2)
203   CONTINUE
      DO 204 I=1,NINT2
      PL(I,6)=DENL(I)
      PL(I,4)=XDEN(I)
204   PL(I,5)=DENP(I)
      TEXTY(1)=8H   REMAIN
      TEXTY(2)=8HING
      YD=YD-3.5
      CALL PLOTB(4.,2.,NINT2,1,TEXTX,TEXTY,SYM,XD,YD)
      IN(1)=6
      YD=YD-3.5
      TEXTY(1)=8H    LOST
      TEXTY(2)=8H
      CALL PLOTB(4.,2.,NINT2,1,TEXTX,TEXTY,SYM,XD,YD)
210   FORMAT(///,1X,"TEMPO/EC",2X,20F6.2)
211   FORMAT(///,1X,"TEMP/EC",3X,20F6.2)
      CALL AVER(NINT,NLEFT,NOR,PES1,SO,XDEN,DENP,DENL,-1)
      IF(NPRT.LT.0) GO TO 223
      PRINT 221,(XDEN(I),I=1,NINT3,2)
      PRINT 222,(DENP(I),I=1,NINT3,2)
221   FORMAT(///,1X,"SO",8X,20F6.2)
222   FORMAT(/,1X,"EKO/EC",4X,20F6.2)
223   CONTINUE
      DO 224 I=1,NINT2
      PL(I,4)=XDEN(I)
224   PL(I,6)=DENP(I)
      TEXTX(2)=8HS
      TEXTY(1)=8HINITIAL
      TEXTY(2)=8HTEMP
      XD=XD+7.2
      YD=YD+7.0
      CALL PLOTB(4.,2.,NINT2,1,TEXTX,TEXTY,SYM,XD,YD)
      CALL AVER(NINT,NLEFT,NOR,PES2,SJ,XDEN,DENP,DENL,1)
      IF(NPRT.LT.0) GO TO 227
      PRINT 225,(XDEN(I),I=1,NINT3,2)
      PRINT 226,(DENP(I),I=1,NINT3,2)
225   FORMAT(///,1X,"S",9X,20F6.2)
226   FORMAT(/,1X,"EK/EC",5X,20F6.2)
227   CONTINUE
      DO 228 I=1,NINT2
      PL(I,4)=XDEN(I)
228   PL(I,6)=DENP(I)
      TEXTX(2)=8HS
      TEXTY(1)=8H    TEMP
      TEXTY(2)=8H
      YD=YD-3.5
      CALL PLOTB(4.,2.,NINT2,1,TEXTX,TEXTY,SYM,XD,YD)
238   CONTINUE
      RETURN
```

```
C
330   FORMAT(/6X,"COLLISION TIME =",F8.2,8X,"PERIODS TRAVERSED =",
     1 F8.1/)
340   FORMAT(///,1X,"S0",8X,20F6.2)
350   FORMAT(/,1X,"DIST REM",2X,20F6.2)
360   FORMAT(/,1X,"DIST LOST",1X,20F6.2)
370   FORMAT(///,1X,"S",9X,20F6.2)
380   FORMAT(///,1X,"ETA0",6X,20F6.2)
390   FORMAT(///,1X,"ETA",7X,20F6.2)
400   FORMAT(///,1X,"PHI0",6X,20F6.2)
410   FORMAT(///28X,"COSINE TEST FUNCTION",/)
420   FORMAT(//30X,"1-S TEST FUNCTION",/)
430   FORMAT(61X,"STANDARD")
440   FORMAT(////,18X,"CONFINEMENT TIME TAU AND LOSS RATE  1/TAU "/)
450   FORMAT(12X,"TIME INTERVAL",11X,"TAU",6X,"LOSS RATE"
     1 ,6X,"DEVIATION",/)
460   FORMAT(5X,"HALF INTERVAL",F7.2,4X,F10.1,5X,F10.3,5X,F10.3)
470   FORMAT(5X,"FULL INTERVAL",F7.2,4X,F10.1,5X,F10.3,5X,F10.3)
480   FORMAT(///25X,"PARTICLE LOSS TEST FUNCTION",/)
490   FORMAT(/,13X,"ENERCON ="E13.3,12X,"CPU TIME ="I6,
     1 "S"/)
500   FORMAT(/26X,"MEAN FREE PATH / FIELD PERIOD =",F8.1,)
510   FORMAT(//05X,"CONFINEMENT TIME ="I4,3X,"EQUIVALENT TO ",
     1 I4," MS AT 1 TESLA")
520   FORMAT(//05X,"ELECTRON CONFINEMENT TIME ="I4,3X,"EQUIVALENT TO "
     1 ,I4," MS AT 1 TESLA")
530   FORMAT(3X,17HEXPONENTIAL DECAY)
540   FORMAT(36HEXPONENTIAL DECAY OF EXPECTED VALUES)
550   FORMAT(10HHISTOGRAMS)
      END



      SUBROUTINE AVER(NINT,NLEFT,NOR,Y,X,XDEN,FS,FL,IND)
C     COMPUTES PARTICLE AVERAGES
      USE NAME3
      DIMENSION X(1),Y(1),XDEN(1),FS(1),FL(1),NS(100),NL(100)
      SLIM=0.99
      IF(IND.LT.0.0) SLIM=10.0
      XMAX=-1.0E10
      XMIN=1.0E10
      DO 1 I=1,NOR
      XMAX=AMAX1(XMAX,X(I))
    1 XMIN=AMIN1(XMIN,X(I))
      X1=0.0
      X2=0.0
      IF(XMAX.GT.0.0) X1=1.0
      IF(XMIN.LT.0.0) X2=1.0
      XMIN=AINT(XMIN)-X2
      XMAX=AINT(XMAX)+X1
      DX=(XMAX-XMIN)/NINT
      X2=XMIN
      DO 5 J=1,NINT
      X1=X2
      FS(2*J-1)=0.0
      FL(2*J-1)=0.0
      NS(J)=0
      NL(J)=0
      X2=X1+DX
      XDEN(2*J-1)=X1
      XDEN(2*J)=X2
      DO 4 I=1,NOR
```

```
        IF(X1.LE.X(I).AND.X(I).LT.X2) GO TO 2
        GO TO 4
      2 IF(SJ(I).GT.SLIM) GO TO 3
        FS(2*J-1)=FS(2*J-1)+Y(I)
        NS(J)=NS(J)+1
        GO TO 4
      3 FL(2*J-1)=FL(2*J-1)+Y(I)
        NL(J)=NL(J)+1
      4 CONTINUE
      5 CONTINUE
        DO 6 J=1,NINT
        IF(NS(J).GT.0)FS(2*J-1)=FS(2*J-1)/NS(J)
        IF(NL(J).GT.0)FL(2*J-1)=FL(2*J-1)/NL(J)
        FS(2*J)=FS(2*J-1)
      6 FL(2*J)=FL(2*J-1)
        FS(2*NINT+1)=0.0
        FL(2*NINT+1)=0.0
        XDEN(2*NINT+1)=XDEN(2*NINT)
        RETURN
        END


        SUBROUTINE DENSITY(NINT,NLEFT,NOR,X,XDEN,FS,FL,IND)
C       DISTRIBUTION FUNCTION
        USE NAME3
        DIMENSION X(1),XDEN(1),FS(1),FL(1)
        SLIM=0.99
        IF(IND.LT.0.0) SLIM=10.0
        XMAX=-1.E10
        XMIN=1.0E10
        DO 1 I=1,NOR
        XMAX=AMAX1(XMAX,X(I))
      1 XMIN=AMIN1(XMIN,X(I))
        X1=0.0
        X2=0.0
        IF(XMAX.GT.0.0) X1=1.0
        IF(XMIN.LT.0.0) X2=1.0
        XMIN=AINT(XMIN)-X2
        XMAX=AINT(XMAX)+X1
        DX=(XMAX-XMIN)/NINT
        X2=XMIN
        DO 5 J=1,NINT
        X1=X2
        FS(2*J-1)=0.0
        FL(2*J-1)=0.0
        X2=X1+DX
        XDEN(2*J-1)=X1
        XDEN(2*J)=X2
        DO 4 I=1,NOR
        IF(X1.LE.X(I).AND.X(I).LT.X2) GO TO 2
        GO TO 4
      2 IF(SJ(I).GT.SLIM) GO TO 3
        FS(2*J-1)=FS(2*J-1)+1.0
        GO TO 4
      3 FL(2*J-1)=FL(2*J-1)+1.0
      4 CONTINUE
      5 CONTINUE
        DO 6 J=1,NINT
        FS(2*J)=FS(2*J-1)
      6 FL(2*J)=FL(2*J-1)
        XDEN(2*NINT+1)=XDEN(2*NINT)
```

```
      FS(2*NINT+1)=0.0
      FL(2*NINT+1)=0.0
      RETURN
      END


      SUBROUTINE SLOPE(I1,I2,I3,EX,DEV)
C     ESTIMATION OF LOSS RATE
      USE NAME15
      NP=I2-I1+1
      A11=FLOAT(NP)
      A12=0.0
      A22=0.0
      B1=0.0
      B2=0.0
      DO 1 I=I1,I2
      B1=B1+PL(I,I3)
      B2=B2+PL(I,I3)*PL(I,10)
      A12=A12+PL(I,10)
    1 A22=A22+PL(I,10)*PL(I,10)
      DET=A11*A22-A12*A12
      X1=(B1*A22-B2*A12)/DET
      X2=(B2*A11-B1*A12)/DET
      EX=-X2
      DEV=0.0
      AV=0.0
      DO 2 I=I1,I2
      AV=AV+PL(I,I3)
      ERR=X1+X2*PL(I,10)-PL(I,I3)
    2 DEV=DEV+ERR*ERR
      AV1=ABS(AV/NP)
      AV1=AMAX1(AV1,1.0E-10)
      DEV=SQRT(DEV/A11)/ABS(AV1)
      RETURN
      END


      SUBROUTINE PLOTB (XL,YL,N,M,TEXTX,TEXTY,SYM,XD,YD)
C     DRIVER FOR PLOT ROUTINES
C     PLOTS PL(I,IN(J)) FOR 0<J<5 AS A FUNCTION OF PL(I,IN(5)).
C     XL AND YL ARE THE LENGTHS IN INCHES OF THE X AND Y AXES. N IS THE
C     NUMBER OF POINTS PLOTTED FOR EACH CURVE, M IS THE NUMBER OF
C     CURVES. TEXTX AND TEXTY ARE THE LABELS FOR THE X AND Y AXES.
C     SYM(J) IS THE LABEL FOR THE J-TH CURVE.
      USE NAME15
      DIMENSION TEXTX(3), TEXTY(3), XA(2), XB(2), SYM(4)
      XMIN=1000000.
      XMAX=-1000000.
      YMAX=-1000000.
      YMIN=1000000.
      DO 10 I=1,N
      XMAX=AMAX1(XMAX,PL(I,IN(5)))
      XMIN=AMIN1(XMIN,PL(I,IN(5)))
      DO 10 J=1,M
      YMAX=AMAX1(YMAX,PL(I,IN(J)))
   10 YMIN=AMIN1(YMIN,PL(I,IN(J)))
      IF (XMAX-XMIN.LE.0.0000001) XMAX=XMIN+0.0000001
      IF (YMAX-YMIN.LE.0.0000001) YMAX=YMIN+0.0000001
   11 CONTINUE
      XA(1)=XMIN
      XA(2)=XMAX
```

```
      XB(1)=YMIN
      XB(2)=YMAX
      CALL GAXIS (XD,YD,XD+XL,YD,0,0,0,"F8.2",3,XA)
      CALL GAXIS (XD,YD,XD,YD+YL,0,0,1,"E8.1",3,XB)
      CALL SETLCH (XD+0.5,YD-0.5,1,0,1,0)
      CALL CRTBCD (TEXTX,3)
      CALL SETLCH (XD-1.2,YD+0.25,1,0,1,1)
      CALL CRTBCD (TEXTY,3)
      XOR=XA(1)
      YO=XB(1)
      DY=(XB(2)-XB(1))/YL
      DX=(XA(2)-XA(1))/XL
      DO 40 J=1,M
      PL1=(PL(1,IN(5))-XOR)/DX+XD
      PL2=(PL(1,IN(J))-YO)/DY+YD
      CALL SETCRT (PL1,PL2)
      DO 30 I=1,N
      PL1=(PL(I,IN(5))-XOR)/DX+XD
      PL2=(PL(I,IN(J))-YO)/DY+YD
   30 CALL VECTOR (PL1,PL2)
      CALL SETLCH (PL1+.1,PL2,1,0,1,0)
      CALL CRTBCD (SYM(J))
   40 CONTINUE
      RETURN
      END


      SUBROUTINE ADDORB
C     ADDITION OF MORE ORBITS
      USE NAME2
      USE NAME3
      USE NAME6
      USE NAME9
      USE NAME11
      USE NAME12
      USE NAME13
      USE NAME14
      USE NAME15
      USE NAME16
      REWIND 3
      REWIND 4
      DO 1 I=1,7000
      READ (3) (PL(I,J),J=1,10)
      IEND=I
      IF (PL(I,1).LT.0.) GO TO 2
    1 CONTINUE
    2 CONTINUE
      READ (3) X1,X2,X3,NM1,NLEFT1,NM3,NOR1,NM4,NM5,NM6
      READ (3) (ETA(KK),AMAG(KK),SO(KK),PSIO(KK),PHIO(KK),SJ(KK),TJ(KK)
     1 ,ETAO(KK),ETAMA(KK),ETAMI(KK),PSIT(KK),PHIT(KK),B(KK),
     2 Y(4*KK-3),Y(4*KK-2),Y(4*KK-1),Y(4*KK),EKINO(KK),EKIN(KK),
     3 POT(KK),EKMAX(KK),EKMIN(KK),ENER(KK),KK=1,NOR1)
      DO 3 I=1,7000
      READ (4) (PL1(I,J),J=1,10)
      IENDA=I
      IF (PL1(I,1).LT.0.) GO TO 4
    3 CONTINUE
    4 IEND=IEND-1
      IENDA=IENDA-1
      READ (4) X1,X2,X3,NM1,NLEFT2,NM3,NOR2,NM4,NM5,NM6
      NOR=NOR1+NOR2
```

```
      NOR3=NOR1+1
      NLEFT=NLEFT1+NLEFT2
      READ (4) (ETA(KK),AMAG(KK),SO(KK),PSIO(KK),PHIO(KK),SJ(KK),TJ(KK)
     1 ,ETAO(KK),ETAMA(KK),ETAMI(KK),PSIT(KK),PHIT(KK),B(KK),
     2 Y(4*KK-3),Y(4*KK-2),Y(4*KK-1),Y(4*KK),EKINO(KK),EKIN(KK),
     3 POT(KK),EKMAX(KK),EKMIN(KK),ENER(KK),KK=NOR3,NOR)
      NLOST=NOR-NLEFT
      IF(PL(IEND,10).GT.PL1(IENDA,10)) GO TO 5
      ITIM=IEND
      DELTC=(PL(IEND,10)-PL(1,10))/(ITIM-1)
      GO TO 6
    5 ITIM=IENDA
      DELTC=(PL1(IENDA,10)-PL1(1,10))/(ITIM-1)
    6 CONTINUE
      TP2(1)=0.
      DO 7 I=2,ITIM
      TP2(I)=TP2(I-1)+DELTC
    7 CONTINUE
      DO 12 K=1,9
      DO 8 I=1,IEND
      TP1(I)=PL(I,10)
    8 FL1(I)=PL(I,K)
      CALL SPLIF(1,IEND,TP1,FL1,P1,P2,P3,3,0.,3,0.,0,0.,IND)
      CALL INTPL(1,ITIM,TP2,PL2,1,IEND,TP1,FL1,P1,P2,P3,MODE)
      DO 9 I=1,ITIM
      PL(I,K)=PL2(I)
    9 CONTINUE
      DO 10 I=1,IENDA
      TP1(I)=PL1(I,10)
   10 FL1(I)=PL1(I,K)
      CALL SPLIF(1,IENDA,TP1,FL1,P1,P2,P3,3,0.,3,0.,0,0.0,IND)
      CALL INTPL(1,ITIM,TP2,PL2,1,IENDA,TP1,FL1,P1,P2,P3,MODE)
      DO 11 I=1,ITIM
      PL1(I,K)=PL2(I)
   11 CONTINUE
   12 CONTINUE
      DO 14 I=1,ITIM
      PL(I,1)=AMAX1(PL(I,1),PL1(I,1))
      PL(I,2)=AMIN1(PL(I,2),PL1(I,2))
      PL(I,3)=(NLEFT1*PL(I,3)+NLEFT2*PL1(I,3))/(NLEFT1+NLEFT2)
      PL(I,4)=PL(I,4)+PL1(I,4)
      PL(I,9)=(NLEFT1*PL(I,9)+NLEFT2*PL1(I,9))/(NLEFT1+NLEFT2)
      DO 13 K=5,8
   13 PL(I,K)=(NOR1*PL(I,K)+NOR2*PL1(I,K))/(NOR1+NOR2)
   14 PL(I,10)=TP2(I)
      REWIND 3
      DO 15 I=1,ITIM
      WRITE (3) (PL(I,K),K=1,10)
   15 CONTINUE
      DO 16 I=1,15
   16 FL(I)=-1.0
      WRITE (3) (FL(I),I=1,10)
      WRITE (3) T1,T2,TSE,NODE,NLEFT,ICOL,NOR,NTER,KTER,INI
      WRITE (3) (ETA(KK),AMAG(KK),SO(KK),PSIO(KK),PHIO(KK),SJ(KK),TJ(KK)
     1 ,ETAO(KK),ETAMA(KK),ETAMI(KK),PSIT(KK),PHIT(KK),B(KK),
     2 Y(4*KK-3),Y(4*KK-2),Y(4*KK-1),Y(4*KK),EKINO(KK),EKIN(KK),
     3 POT(KK),EKMAX(KK),EKMIN(KK),ENER(KK),KK=1,NOR)
      RETURN
      END
```

```
      SUBROUTINE ELPOT(Y)
C     EVALUATION OF THE ELECTRIC POTENTIAL
C     THE ELECTRIC POTENTIAL, POT, IS A FUNCTION OF THE THREE
C     VARIABLES PHI, PSI, AND S, REPRESENTED IN THE CODE BY Y(4*I-1),
C     Y(4*I-2), AND Y(4*I-3) RESPECTIVELY. EACH TERM CONTRIBUTING
C     TO POT CONTAINS THE FACTOR EC=0.5*RADL*RADL.
C     THE DERIVATIVES OF POT WITH RESPECT TO S, PHI AND PSI MUST
C     ALSO BE COMPUTED HERE.
      USE NAME2
      USE NAME9
      USE NAME11
      USE NAME12
      USE NAME14
      EOC=E0*EC
      XE0=1.0
      XE1=XE0*EOC
      SHFT1=E1*EC
      SHFT2=E2*EC
      SHFT3=E3*EC
      DO 1 I=1,NLEFT
    1 PES2(I)=AMIN1(Y(4*I-3),0.999)
      DO 3 I=1,NLEFT
      POT(I)=EOC*((1.0-PES2(I))**XE0-(1.0-S0(I))**XE0)
     1 +SHFT3*(COS(17.*Y(4*I-2)+12.0*Y(4*I-1))-COS(17.*PSI0(I)+12.0*
     2 PHI0(I)))
      POTS(I)=-XE1*(1.0-PES2(I))**(XE0-1.0)
      POTPH(I)=-12.0*SHFT3*SIN(17.*Y(4*I-2)+12.*Y(4*I-1))
    3 POTPS(I)=-17.*SHFT3*SIN(17.*Y(4*I-2)+12.*Y(4*I-1))
      RETURN
      END
```